**W9-AXG-822**

CULTURE SMART!

# KOREA

## THE ESSENTIAL GUIDE TO CUSTOMS & CULTURE

JAMES HOARE

WITH A CONTRIBUTION ON POPULAR CULTURE
BY DOORI POWER

KUPERARD

"The real voyage of discovery consists not in
seeking new landscapes, but in having new eyes."

Adapted from Marcel Proust, *Remembrance of Things Past.*

ISBN 978 1 78702 888 3

British Library Cataloguing in Publication Data
A CIP catalogue entry for this book is available
from the British Library

First published in Great Britain
by Kuperard, an imprint of Bravo Ltd
59 Hutton Grove, London N12 8DS
Tel: +44 (0) 20 8446 2440
www.culturesmart.co.uk
Inquiries: publicity@kuperard.co.uk

Design Bobby Birchall
Printed in Turkey by Elma Basım

# ABOUT THE AUTHOR

**JAMES HOARE** spent over thirty years in the British Diplomatic Service, which included postings to Seoul and Beijing. As *Chargé d'Affaires*, he established the British Embassy in Pyongyang, North Korea. He has a Ph.D. in East Asian history and has written extensively on China, Japan, and the two Koreas. His books include *Embassies in the East: The Story of the British and their Embassies in China, Japan and Korea from 1859 to the Present*; *Historical Dictionary of the Republic of Korea*; *Historical Dictionary of the Democratic People's Republic of Korea*; and with his wife, Susan Pares, *Korea: An Introduction*; *Conflict in Korea: An Encyclopedia*; and *North Korea in the 21st Century: An Interpretative Guide*.

Dr. Hoare is a regular guest on radio and television. He is an Associate Fellow at the Royal Institute of International Affairs (Chatham House), and an Honorary Research Associate, Centre of Korean Studies, School of Oriental and African Studies, University of London. He is a past president of the Royal Asiatic Society, Korea Branch, and of the British Association for Korean Studies.

## COVID-19

The coronavirus pandemic of 2020 affected millions of people around the world, causing unprecedented social and economic disruption. As the impact of this global crisis continues to unfold, in many countries social norms are being challenged, and enduring changes will be reflected in future editions of Culture Smart! titles.

# CONTENTS

# MAP OF KOREA

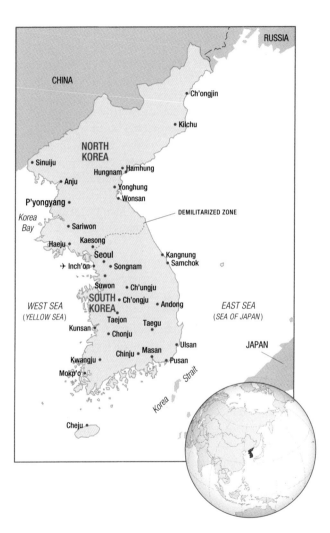

# INTRODUCTION

The twentieth century was not kind to the people of the Korean peninsula. In 1905 Japan's defeat of Russia paved the way for the Japanese protectorate in Korea. Then in 1910, the Japanese annexed Korea as a full-scale colony. Liberation in 1945 brought not independence as all Koreans had hoped, but the division of the peninsula that has lasted until today. North Korea attempted to reunify Korea by force in 1950. Outside intervention saved both Korean states from extinction, but the war intensified the division.

Only after 1998 was there any significant and sustained move to heal the wounds of the past, and that only lasted ten years. Since 2018, there have been signs of a possible improvement in relations between the two Koreas but there is a long way to go. The issue is complicated by the very different conditions of the two Koreas. The North remains a dictatorship, and having once led in economic development and industrialization, is in economic decline. The South, by contrast, once viewed as an economic disaster ruled by authoritarians, built a modern economy in the 1960s and 1970s, weathered the financial storms of the 1990s, and seems well on the road to democracy. The two Koreas are now interacting as never before. Major issues remain, such as the role of outside powers and North Korea's pursuit of a nuclear weapons program. Yet the future again looks more positive than it has for years.

The 1988 Seoul Olympics and the 2002 World Cup, shared with Japan, helped to increase knowledge about South Korea, but have not overcome widespread ignorance about the Korean people and their culture. Yet those who visit Korea, whether North or South, will find a place of great interest with much to offer. Koreans, when not constrained by politics or other considerations, are friendly and sociable. The peninsula has areas of outstanding natural beauty. The South's cities, if not always beautiful, are vibrant and alive. The North, while very different, is well worth getting to know.

*Culture Smart! Korea* shows how Koreans think and act, the pitfalls to avoid, and introduces some of the delights of the peninsula. It is the product of an involvement that stretches back to the early 1970s, and of my residence in both North and South Korea. It derives partly from a little book called *Simple Guide to Korea: Customs and Etiquette*, which my wife and I wrote. The European Department of the North Korean Ministry of Foreign Affairs, to whom we gave a copy, told us that this had been made required reading for all the staff of the department, since it provided real insights into Korean thinking and behavior. I hope that *Culture Smart! Korea* will do the same for many other readers.

| | | |
|---|---|---|
| **Official Name** | Republic of Korea | *Daehan minguk* |
| **Capital City** | Seoul | Pop. 10.4 million |
| **Major Cities** | Inch'on, Taejon, Taegu, Pusan, Kwangju, Ulsan | |
| **Area** | 38,131 sq. miles (98,759 sq. km) | |
| **Climate** | Continental, tempered by maritime influences | |
| **Population** | 51 million (2019) | |
| **Ethnic Makeup** | Korean: 100% | |
| **Government** | Democracy, with executive president and unicameral legislature (National Assembly) | |
| **Borders** | Demilitarized Zone between North and South Korea: 151 miles (240 km) | |
| **Currency** | Won, divided into 100 chon, but the latter has gone out of usage. The South Korean won has a different exchange value from the North. | Coins are Won 1, 5, 50, 100, and 500. The first two have practically disappeared. Notes are Won 1,000, 5,000, and 10,000. |
| **Language** | Korean. People who attended school before August 1945 will have learned Japanese. | |
| **Religion** | Traditional: Buddhism, shamanism, and Confucianism. Since the eighteenth century, Christianity has grown, and over a quarter of the population is now Christian. There are a number of new religions, and Islam has about 40,000 followers. | |
| **Media** | Thriving press, radio, and TV. Widespread use of computers, the Internet, and cell phones. There are three English-language dailies: *Korea Herald*, *Korea Times*, and the *Joongang Ilbo* supplement to the International *Herald Tribune*. | |
| **Internet Domain** | .kr | |
| **Electricity** | 220 v, although some 110 v outlets may still be found. US-style plugs are the norm. | |
| **Time** | GMT + 8 | |

| Official Name | Democratic People's Republic of Korea | *Choson minjujui inmin konghwaguk* |
|---|---|---|
| **Capital City** | Pyongyang | Pop. 2 million |
| **Major Cities** | Nampo, Kaesong, Wonsan, Shinuiju, Hamhung | |
| **Area** | 46,768 sq. miles (121,129 sq. km) | |
| **Climate** | Continental, tempered by maritime influences | |
| **Population** | 25 million (2019) | |
| **Ethnic Makeup** | Korean: 100% | |
| **Government** | Authoritarian dictatorship, with unicameral legislature (Supreme People's Assembly) | |
| **Borders** | Demilitarized Zone between North and South Korea: 151 miles (240 km). Border with People's Republic of China: 640 miles (1,025 km); and with Russia: 9 miles (15 km) | |
| **Currency** | Won, divided into 100 chon. The North Korean won has a different exchange value from the South Korean won. Foreigners are no longer barred from using North Korean currency, but more usual is paymnent in dollars, Euros, Japanese Yen, or Chinese renminbi. | |
| **Language** | Korean. People who attended school before August 1945 will have learned Japanese. | |
| **Religion** | North Korea is an atheist state. It is officially acknowledged that there are Buddhists, Roman Catholics, and Protestant Christians, and followers of a Korean religion, Chondogyo. | |
| **Media** | All media outlets are state or party controlled. The main newspaper is the party journal *Rodong Shinmun* (Worker's Daily). The English-language *Pyongyang Times* is a weekly. There are also editions in a number of other languages. | |
| **Internet Domain** | .kp | |
| **Electricity** | 220 v. US-style plugs are the norm. | |
| **Time** | GMT + 8 | |

# CHAPTER ONE

# LAND & PEOPLE

The Korean peninsula has been occupied by two independent states since 1948: the Democratic People's Republic of Korea (DPRK, known as North Korea) in the northern part, and the Republic of Korea (ROK, known as South Korea) in the south. The peninsula curves out from the landmass of Northeast Asia, separating the Yellow Sea between China and the peninsula from what the Koreans call the East Sea. The latter title is disputed by Japan, which calls this stretch of water the Sea of Japan. To the north, there is a long land border with China, and a short one with Russia. The border is ill-defined in places, and Korean and Chinese claims overlap. Between the two Koreas, the 38th parallel originally formed the boundary as set by Soviet and US occupation forces in 1945. Now there is a Demilitarized Zone (DMZ), established by the July 27, 1953, Korean Armistice that marked the end of the Korean War (1950–53). This zone, 2.5 miles (4 km) wide, stretches some 151 miles (243 km) on land and another 37 miles (59.5 km) through the Han River estuary, right across the peninsula. Despite the area's official title, both sides brought weapons into their respective sectors from the very start of the armistice, and the DMZ, ironically, has been one of the most fortified regions in the world. For years it was virtually impassable. Prisoner of war exchanges took place in 1953. From 1971 to '73, there were North–South delegations that crossed, but it was not until after 2000 that such crossings became frequent. For a brief period there were tourists' visits from South to North. The improved relationship since the beginning of 2018 may lead to their resumption. One positive side effect of the DMZ is that much wildlife finds a peaceful sanctuary there, despite the occasional loss to a landmine or

*Dream Journey to the Peach Blossom Land.* Painting on silk scroll by Ahn Gyeon, 1447.

weapons tripwire. Some 1,600 plant and animal species have been identified as living in the DMZ, including the rare white crane. There have even been suggestions of turning it into a "peace park."

## GEOGRAPHY

The peninsula is rugged, with Mount Paektu, in North Korea on the Sino–Korean border, reaching 9,003 feet (2,744 m), while the highest mountain on the South Korean mainland is Mount Chiri in the Sobaek range, at 6,250 feet (1,905 m). Mount Halla on Cheju Island, the highest mountain in South Korea, is 6,365 feet (1,937 m). The whole peninsula is divided by a series of mountain ranges. It is spectacularly beautiful in places, with jagged peaks and fast-flowing streams. This beauty has long been reflected in Korean painting.

The total area of the peninsula is about 85,328 square miles (220,998 sq. km), or roughly the size of mainland Britain. The mountain ranges leave relatively little land for cultivation. Farming and habitation are confined to about 16–20 percent of the total land area. As both Koreas have industrialized since the 1950s, so the amount of land available has steadily shrunk. The heaviest population concentrations have always been on the western side of the peninsula, which also has the best farmland.

There are about 3,500 islands, though some of these are disappearing as both Koreas have compensated for their lack of land by reclaiming it from the sea, a process that originally began in the Japanese colonial period (1910–45). Seoul's new airport at Inch'on, opened in 2000, is built on a mixture of islands and reclaimed land. The east coast has steep cliffs and few islands, and the waters are deep. Far out to sea is Ullung-do, a popular tourist destination, famous for squid fishing. Even further to the east is a small crop of rocks known as Tok-to in Korean, and Takeshima in Japanese, whose ownership is disputed between both Koreas and Japan. (Even more obscurely, they appear on many Western maps as the Liancourt Rocks, named after a nineteenth-century French survey vessel.) Tok-to is currently occupied by a detachment of South Korean police. The dispute flares up from time to time as one side or the other engages in a provocative

Rugged coastline on Cheju Island.

action or issues an inflammatory statement, then fades back into obscurity for a bit.

On the western side, the sea is shallow, with numerous islands and high tidal variations. This produces good fishing, which leads to clashes between vessels from the two Koreas and from China. Off the southern coast, drowned valleys have produced many islands, creating another area of spectacular natural beauty, with several national parks. Further off is the island of Cheju, South Korea's only island province. Its subtropical climate and subtly different traditions have made it a popular vacation spot since the 1950s. Before Koreans had the opportunity to go overseas on such occasions, it was the main honeymoon destination. Now large numbers of Koreans still visit, but a visa-free regime has encouraged many other visitors as well. These include many Chinese, which has led to some local concern. Cheju has also attracted some foreign schools, including the North London Collegiate School.

Little remains of the original deciduous forests that once covered the peninsula, now replaced by cultivated land or secondary forest. Rice paddy is the most widespread form of cultivation, even in the northern part of the peninsula, which is not well suited to it. Other grains include wheat and barley, and potatoes are now widely grown in North Korea. In the South, the use of plastic sheeting has greatly increased the supply of winter vegetables. There is some use of it in the North, partly encouraged by foreign aid workers, but it is expensive, and less used than in the South. Cheju's subtropical climate led to the development of a citrus fruit industry in the 1970s.

## CLIMATE

The climate is varied; semitropical in Cheju, where oranges will grow, but in the rest of the peninsula varying from sub-zero winter temperatures to summer monsoons. Occasionally, winters can be particularly hard. In the north of the peninsula in January 2001, for example, temperatures briefly plunged below -58°F (-50°C), the coldest they had been for fifty years. December 2011 also saw another very cold spell. Usually, winters are more moderate, though there are regular spells of below-zero temperatures between November and March. Visitors to South Korea will find that buildings are well heated in winter, so getting the right balance of clothing is not always easy. In North Korea, however, while individual hotel rooms will be warm, few public buildings, even hotels, can supply adequate heating in winter, so it is necessary to bundle up well.

## A BRIEF HISTORY

### The Three Kingdoms

Koreans trace their historical origins back to the Neolithic age (c. 5000–1000 BCE), when the mythical founder of the Korean state, the half-human, half-divine Tan'gun, is supposed to have flourished. (Tan'gun is regarded as the ancestor of all Koreans, and in the 1990s, in one of the ongoing rounds in the competition for legitimacy between the two Koreas, the North Koreans claimed to have discovered his tomb near Pyongyang.) The reality is that it was only much later, well after the beginning of the Christian era, that the first recognizable states emerged on the peninsula. These are known as the Three Kingdoms, of Koguryo, Paekche, and Shilla. All were heavily influenced by developments both political and cultural in China. For a time, the Chinese empire had commanderies, or military colonies, on what is now Korean territory. The greatest of these was Lelang or Lolang (Nangnang in Korean), established around 108 BCE in the area near modern Pyongyang. Koguryo overthrew it in 313 CE.

### Claiming the Past

As an example of how the past continually intrudes into the present in East Asia, a dispute simmers between Chinese and South Korean academics about whether Koguryo was, in fact, a Sinic kingdom, and thus to be considered as part of China's history, or, as the Koreans would argue, a proto-Korean kingdom. The dispute arose following a Chinese government intervention to block a North Korean attempt to register certain Koguryo tomb sites with UNESCO as World Heritage Sites. North Korea, heavily dependent on China, chose not to publicize the issue, but South Korean scholars, backed eventually by their government, had no such inhibitions. Separate Chinese and North Korean proposals for the registration of their respective groups of tombs as World Heritage Sites succeeded in June 2004.

### Unified Korea

In 668 CE, Shilla succeeded in uniting most of the peninsula, thus helping to create a sense of identity among the peoples on the Korean peninsula that was separate and distinct from that of the Chinese to the north. Shilla's capital was at Kyongju, in the southeast of the peninsula, where there are still splendid archaeological remains to testify to its cultural richness. It was also during this period that Buddhism, also introduced from China,

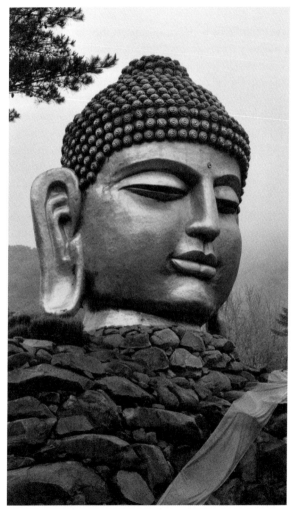

Golden Buddha head at the entrance of Wowoo Temple, South Korea.

truly flourished in the peninsula. At the same time, the Koreans were absorbing Confucian teachings from China. Shilla was succeeded by Koryo (918–1392), from which, through China, the West learned the name "Korea." Under the Koryo dynasty, whose capital was at Kaesong, now in North Korea, Buddhism become the religion of the court and the aristocracy. Also during this period, Korea made many advances in military science, especially in the use of rockets and other explosives, and began the development of printing. Raids by Chinese bandits and Japanese pirates in the late fourteenth century increased the importance of the military, which for a time dominated government. But following disputes over how to react to dynastic changes in China that saw the overthrow of the Mongol dynasty by the Ming, one general, Yi Song Gye, staged a coup d'état, and proclaimed himself king of a new Chosun dynasty in 1392.

The Chosun, or Yi, dynasty ruled Korea until 1910. The capital was moved from Kaesong to Hanyang (modern Seoul), which became, and remained, the economic, social, and political center of the country until the division of the 1940s. It then became the capital of South Korea but remained formally the capital of the North also until 1972. Under the Yi, Buddhism fell from favor, to be replaced by Confucianism, also imported from China. This new philosophy, with its strong emphasis on social order and education, came to dominate most aspects of Korean life, and its influence can still be traced today. Buddhism never vanished entirely from the scene. In theory, the monks were banished from the cities into remote mountain areas. Even today, most of South Korea's major Buddhist temples

Sejong "the Great," fourth king of the Chosun dynasty.

are to be found in hills and remote valleys, though the expansion of the cities has brought others back into urban areas. Many kings, even those who persecuted Buddhists, turned to the religion in old age, and it was always strong among the women of the court. Among ordinary people too, Buddhism, with its pantheons of those willing to assist mere mortals, proved more alluring in times of personal distress or general troubles than the more austere doctrines of the Confucians.

## Foreign Pressure

Unrest in Korea's neighbors, China and Japan, brought problems for Korea. In the late sixteenth century, under the warlord Hideyoshi Toyotomi (1536–98), the Japanese sought to use the peninsula as a path to conquer China, a move that turned into the long drawn-out Imjin wars. The conflicts, from 1592 to 1593 and again from 1597 to 1598, led to Chinese intervention, which saved Korea.

Painting of the defense of Busanjin Fortress, 1760.

The wars also produced Korea's greatest hero, Admiral Yi Sun Shin, but the fighting left Korea devastated. Large numbers of Koreans were killed or captured. Skilled craftsmen, especially potters, were carted off to Japan, where they helped revitalize the Japanese ceramic industry. Many monasteries and palaces were destroyed at this time and remained in ruins for several hundred years. Korea suffered again as the Manchu seized control of China and its dependencies in the 1630s and 1640s, who demanded subservience to their rule. The Koreans acquiesced, but this left its scars.

It was hardly surprising, therefore, that Korea tended to turn in upon itself from the seventeenth century onward, although this should not be exaggerated. Formal contacts were maintained with both China and Japan, with exchanges of diplomatic missions. It was through such missions to China that new intellectual trends flowed in, including Roman Catholicism, which would provoke bitter persecutions in the nineteenth

Korean tribute bearers in Beijing, 1871.

century. In general, the Koreans sought to be left alone. The scholar-officials, versed in Neo-Confucianism, despised trade and those who demanded it. The country was thus poorly placed to resist the Western and Japanese pressure that began to build up from the 1860s onward. Two wars, the Sino–Japanese War of 1894–95 and the Russo–Japanese War of 1904–05, were fought over the issue of which country should control Korea. Japan won both. Other powers showed little interest in the peninsula after 1905, when Japan proclaimed a British India-style protectorate over Korea. This was followed by outright annexation in 1910.

## Japanese Colonial Rule

There followed thirty-five years of harsh colonial rule until the end of the Second World War brought liberation in 1945. All development in the Korean peninsula from 1910 until 1945 was subordinate to the needs of Japan, a trend that grew worse as the Japanese Empire moved onto an all-out war footing after 1937. The Second World War also led to an intensification of the Japanese campaign to assimilate Koreans into the Japanese Empire. Teaching of the Korean language was forbidden, and Koreans were compelled to take Japanese names.

The Koreans did not endure these developments without opposition. "Righteous armies" opposed the protectorate. On March 1, 1919, Koreans, inspired by President Wilson's rhetoric and hopeful of Western support in the aftermath of the First World War, rose up in a nationwide protest against Japanese rule. The Japanese quelled this uprising with much ferocity. Further anti-Japanese protests would occur sporadically, right up to the eve of the Second World War. Koreans in China and elsewhere organized governments-in-exile, but their activities were often marked more by factionalism than agreement. In the north of the country and in China, Communist-inspired guerrilla groups fought against the Japanese from the late 1920s onward. A massive Japanese military campaign starting in 1939 drove most of these groups into the Soviet Union or deeper into Chinese territory, from which they would emerge in 1945.

## Korea Divided

Korean hopes for the restoration of a unified independent state were not realized. The peninsula was divided into Soviet and American zones, originally for the purpose of taking the Japanese surrender. But the wartime allies could not agree on the future of Korea, and their negotiations broke down, leading eventually to the emergence of two separate states in 1948, the Democratic People's Republic of Korea (North Korea) and the Republic of Korea (South Korea). Neither wanted the continuation of the division, and there was much jockeying for position along the 38th parallel, the formal dividing line between the two states. In June 1950, North Korea launched an all-out attack in an attempt at unification by force. It nearly succeeded but was stopped by United Nations intervention. In the end, after much suffering and great losses, the Korean War only succeeded in perpetuating the division, which still exists today.

## THE KOREAN WAR

The Korean War began with a massive North Korean attack along the 38th parallel on the morning of Sunday, June 25, 1950. South Korean forces, many of them on leave, were not prepared for this, and quickly fell back. Seoul, the capital, fell within three days, and the South Korean government retreated first to Taejon, then to Taegu, and finally to Pusan.

The North Korean forces swept all before them. Although, in the absence of the Soviet Union from the Security Council, the United States quickly rallied United Nations support for the Republic of Korea, this took time to arrive. Some American units were brought in from Japan, but they were lightly armed and proved no match for the North Korean tanks. By August, however, the situation had improved. The North Korean lines were heavily extended, and the line along the Naktong River—the Pusan perimeter—held.

This allowed time for the arrival of more UN forces; the first British troops arrived at the end of August 1950, for example, although British warships had already seen action by then. At the same time, the UN Supreme Commander, General Douglas MacArthur, the head of the Allied occupation forces in Japan, had decided on an ambitious plan for an amphibious landing at Inch'on, the port of Seoul. This began on September 8, 1950, and at the same time, UN forces began to break out of the Pusan perimeter.

MacArthur's forces met little resistance once they had stormed ashore at Inch'on. By then, the North Korean forces were tired and very extended. While there was some fierce fighting as the UN forces moved up the peninsula, the North Korean victories of June and August were now reversed. UN forces soon reached the Han River near Seoul, and then the 38th parallel. They did not stop but pressed on into North Korea. By late October, the South Korean forces had reached the Yalu River, on the border with China, and UN forces were pressing hard behind them.

US infantry manning an M26 Pershing tank in September 1950.

The Chinese had been warning since the crossing of the parallel that they would be prepared to intervene. MacArthur discounted such warnings, but the Chinese began infiltrating forces into Korea. On October 26, 1950, the Chinese struck. Before long, UN forces were in headlong retreat. Some units fought a rearguard action but many just "bugged out," jettisoning supplies and equipment as they fled from the Chinese "hordes." (One story has it that at a UN forces press conference, where the briefing officer had repeatedly talked about the Chinese "hordes," one journalist asked how many made up a normal horde. The term then disappeared from official briefings.)

By January 1951, Seoul had fallen to the Chinese and North Korean forces, and UN troops were south of the Han River. Under the guidance of General Matthew Ridgeway, the UN forces regrouped and began a counterattack. In April, Chinese attempts to drive them further back failed. Seoul was recaptured and he Chinese and North Korean forces were driven back to the 38th parallel.

In April 1951, President Truman dismissed General MacArthur for ignoring instructions. MacArthur would later blame the British for his dismissal, but the reality was that he had overreached himself, and the president was no longer prepared to let him get away with overt criticism of Washington's policies. Ridgeway replaced him.

The war now settled into a stalemate, roughly where it had begun. The fighting continued, but now it was more akin to the trench warfare of the First World War than to the earlier war of movement. Truce negotiations began in the summer of 1951. They were soon adjourned, and it would be two long years before an armistice was agreed to in July 1953. At the last minute, the armistice agreement was almost jeopardized by the South Korean president, Rhee Syngman. Not only did he refuse to sign but he also arranged for the release of large numbers of North Korean prisoners. But despite protests, the agreement came into force on July 27, 1953. It remains in place to this day.

## POSTWAR RECOVERY

Recovery from the Korean War took time. Both Korean states were devastated by the conflict. Three million Koreans were killed, wounded or missing, while 10 million families, one third of the population of the peninsula, were broken up. Thirteen million Koreans, or 43 percent of the population in 1950, were directly affected by the war. The damage was particularly fierce in North Korea, which bore the brunt of the fighting after September 1950, and which was effectively without air cover except in certain remote areas. According to US statistics, the United States Air Force used 386,037 tons of bombs, 32,357 tons of napalm, 313,600 rockets, and 167 million machine-gun rounds against the North.

The North Korean economy was totally destroyed, having lost 8,700 industrial plants, 906,500 acres of farmland, 600,000 houses, 5,000 schools, 1,000 hospitals, and 260 theaters. In 1953, the North's national income was 69.4 percent of that of 1950, electricity production 17.2 percent of 1949, and coal production 17.7 percent of 1949. There had been a huge loss of able-bodied men, who had either been killed or fled to South Korea.

South Korea was also in a bad way. It had lost 17,000 plants, businesses, and factories, 4,000 schools, and 600,000 homes, and GNP had declined by 14 percent during the war. Total property damage was estimated at US $2 billion, about the same as the country's total GNP in 1949. Effectively, therefore, apart from the end of the fighting, both sides found themselves in the summer of 1953 with nothing to mark and nothing to celebrate. For both North and South Korea, such victories as there had been were won by others.

From 1953 onward, the two Koreas concentrated on rebuilding. Both professed their commitment to unification. In reality neither did anything to bring this about. North Korea recovered more quickly than South Korea, aided by massive support from the Soviet Union and its allies, and from China. By the early 1960s, North Korea was well on the way to becoming the second-most industrialized country in Asia, after Japan. It would maintain this lead into the 1970s, but thereafter began to fall behind. A system based on exhortation and overexploitation of both the workforce and machinery could not continue to produce indefinitely. At the same time, agriculture began to suffer from similar problems; the land could not sustain the constant demand for production. These economic difficulties would remain hidden until the collapse of the Soviet Union and its related economic system, for North Korea continued to receive much aid from this source until 1991.

**The North**

Politically North Korea also appeared the more successful of the two Koreas, but at a huge cost. Kim Il Sung used the war to consolidate his power, a process that continued into the postwar years. By the early 1960s there was no one to challenge his preeminence, and he would be the ruler of North Korea until his death in 1994. His eldest son, Kim Jong Il, who was probably born in Russia in 1941 or 1942, then succeeded him. But the younger Kim did not assume his father's role exactly. In a move that struck the outside world as bizarre,

The Eternal President and the Great Leader together.

the deceased elder Kim became the eternal president.
For a time even letters appointing ambassadors were
issued in his name, until countries began to object.
Even today North Korean officials behave as though
Kim Il Sung were still guiding the state.

The younger Kim was more reclusive. His role as
Chairman of the Defense Committee would eventually
be defined as the highest office of the state, and he
became General Secretary of the Korean Workers'
Party, though in a somewhat unorthodox way. But he
did not occupy the forefront of the stage as his father
did. His trips abroad were to Russia and China, and by
train—he was believed to have a fear of flying. He may
also have preferred not to use the elderly former Soviet
aircraft that largely made up the DPRK's civil aviation
fleet until 2008 or 2009. He met few foreigners and gave
no interviews. Kim's own reclusiveness and apparent
suspicion of the outside world are reflected in North
Korean society generally. Few people have traveled

Visitors showing respect before the statues of Kim Il Sung and Kim Jong Il in Pyongyang.

abroad or have access to outside information. With its constant exhortations for vigilance against the enemy, regular air-raid practices, and violent propaganda, North Korea seems trapped in a hostile past.

Kim Jong Il's succession in 1994 also coincided with major economic difficulties. The disappearance of the Soviet Union and its allies had been a major blow. China continued to provide economic support, but periodically indicated that it would not do so forever. Attempts to attract foreign investment proved unsuccessful. Then, in the mid-1990s, a series of natural disasters struck the country. Floods, tidal waves, and drought took a heavy toll on an already weakened economy from 1995 to 1998. The DPRK, in desperation, appealed for international aid. This was forthcoming, but the presence of aid workers, with new ideas and new approaches, led to much tension. Some of the big international organizations, such as Oxfam, pulled out. Many smaller aid groups and the United Nations agencies stayed, but there were constant tensions as the country suffered famine conditions.

These were also the years that saw growing international concern over the possibility of North Korea developing nuclear weapons. The crisis was averted in 1994, partly by the intervention of former United States President Jimmy Carter. It would rear up again in 2002. In 2006 international tension reached a new height after the North's first nuclear test. Despite sanctions, the nuclear program and the parallel development to create an effective means of delivery have continued ever since. It continues to dominate much thinking about the Korean peninsula.

By 2000, the worst of the famine was over. The world was then astonished by a summit meeting between Kim Jong Il and the South Korean president, Kim Dae Jung, the first ever such meeting in the two countries' history. For a moment, it looked as though the two Koreas were on the verge of an historic breakthrough. The moment passed, and although the two sides continued to develop links, the high hopes of 2000 have not yet been fulfilled. The election of Lee Myung Bak as South Korean president brought a more conservative administration to power in 2008. Lee was succeeded by another conservative, Park Geun Hye. Together with the ongoing nuclear issue, these developments saw a major downturn in inter-Korean relations.

Kim Il Sung worked hard to prepare Kim Jong Il to take over the leadership role. The latter, however, seems to have made no preparations for his own successor until he suffered a stroke in 2008. As he recovered and began to appear in public, he was often accompanied by a young man named as Kim Jong Un. Although he was not formally identified in the North Korean media, Kim Jong Un's remarkable similarity to his grandfather, Kim Il Sung, and his apparent ease in the presence of Kim Jong Il, made it clear who he was and the role expected of him. His elevation to the rank of four-star general in 2010 pointed in the same direction. When Kim Jong Il's death from a heart attack was announced in December 2011, formal designation as the successor came soon afterward.

## Kim Jong Un

Kim Jong Un came to power without the long years of training that his father had received. Like his siblings, he had been educated in Switzerland. Kim Jong Il had kept his family out of the public eye and little was known about the new leader. Many speculated that he would be only a figurehead. The powerful team that seemed to have been assembled to guide him, which included several senior military figures and his uncle by marriage, Jang Sang Taek, were believed to be the real power holders. This was soon shown to be a mistaken impression. The new leader quickly began to assert himself. Within a couple of years of his father's death, the group who had followed his coffin had been dismissed. Some, including Jang Sang Taek, were dead, others banished. While paying lip service to his father's memory, the younger Kim shifted power from the army back to the party. By the time a new constitution was adopted in 2016, the National Defense Commission had been replaced by the State Affairs Commission as the highest organ of the state.

Kim also put new emphasis on the nuclear program, ignoring international protests and the increasingly tightening sanctions regime, now also being enforced by Russia and China. By the end of 2017, the North claimed to have both a hydrogen bomb and the means of delivering it to the United States. This led to heated exchanges, threats of war, and mutual name calling between Kim and US President Donald Trump. Then there was a change. Kim all along claimed that there would be a two-pronged approach, with nuclear and economic development going together. There had indeed been some economic efforts between 2011 and 2017, much initially related to the centenary of Kim Il Sung's birth in 2012. The result was new building, especially in Pyongyang, and expenditure on grandiose projects such as ski resorts and a new international airport at Wonsan on the East Coast. But Kim's 2018 New Year Address promised more.

It also reached out to the South Korean president, Moon Jae In. Kim offered to send a team to the 2018 Winter Olympics, due in South Korea in February 2018. From this followed a summit proposal and, to much surprise, an offer to meet Donald Trump. By the end of 2018, Kim and Moon had met not once but three times, relations had been improved with China, and the first ever meeting between an incumbent American president and a North Korean leader took place in Singapore in June. Many problems remained unresolved but there had certainly been change. And Kim had shown that he was no puppet.

Kim Jong Un meets Donald Trump in Singapore.

## The South

Many dismissed South Korea in the years immediately after the Korean War as an economic failure—the term "basket case" was common. Per capita income was very low, at about US $60 per annum. President Rhee Syngman was little interested in economic matters, and content to rely on international handouts. These propped up the system rather than aided economic development.

A student-led uprising ousted Rhee in 1960, when political corruption finally proved too much for the people to bear. After a brief "democratic" interlude, the army seized power in May 1961. South Korea would remain under military dominance until the election of Kim Young Sam as president in 1992.

At first the soldiers had little in the way of plans for the future beyond preventing what they saw as dangerous student overtures to North Korea. Their eventual leader, General Park Chung Hee, had trained at the Japanese Military Academy in the Japanese puppet state of "Manchukuo" in Manchuria and had been an officer in the Imperial Japanese Army in the Second World War. He had been accused of being a Communist in the 1940s but had survived. Park was tough and determined. While he eventually "civilianized" himself and was elected president, there was no doubt that under him military virtues came first.

Park set himself the task of turning South Korea from a basket case into a modern economic power. He had no blueprint and there were several false steps along the way. While presented as capitalism, this was capitalism with a difference. Economic planning, such as the Japanese had used in Manchukuo, was one tool; another was a powerful coercive state, very much on the side of big business.

By the late 1970s South Korea had been transformed from a primarily agricultural country into an industrialized one, well able to match its northern neighbor. Park's assassination by his chief of security in October 1979 caused a momentary pause in this surge, but it resumed under another military leader, Chun Doo Hwan, and continued until the Asian economic crisis of 1997. This, too, proved to be a short-lived problem, and the ROK quickly resumed and has maintained its position as a leading economic power, with an increasing concentration on high-tech consumer goods.

The cornerstone of Park's foreign policy was a good relationship with the United States. To this end, he sent troops to Vietnam in support of American efforts there. He also set out to improve South Korea's virtually nonexistent relations with Japan. The two countries finally established diplomatic relations in 1965, after some thirteen years of negotiations. For the first ten years of his rule, Park pursued a hostile policy toward the North, a policy reciprocated by that country.

In 1971, however, Park made the first overtures to North Korea since the end of the Korean War, a move prompted by the United States' improved relations with China and the Soviet Union. Both North and South found that their principal allies were talking to their principal enemies, and in such circumstances seem to have concluded that it was better to talk to each other in case the great powers once again sacrificed the Korean peninsula for their own purposes. The talks led to the July 4, 1972 Joint Declaration, which held out the hope of a reduction of tensions on the peninsula.

These hopes petered out. Claiming that closer links with the North required strong domestic control, Park set out to reinforce the authoritarian nature of his regime. His successors would try to maintain this position while also trying to improve relations with the North, but it was not until the election of Kim Dae Jung in 1997 that a real breakthrough came. Even if the high hopes raised then did not last, the relationship between the two Koreas for a time changed beyond all recognition.

For some years there were widespread exchanges between the two Korean states. But the continued presence of large military forces on both sides of the Demilitarized Zone shows that many of the old suspicions remained, reinforced by the North's nuclear program. In addition, in 2010, the sinking of a South Korean naval vessel in March, and the shelling of a South Korean island that led to four deaths later in the year, shows that tensions remain high. That said, not all the gains of recent years have been lost. The Kaesong Industrial Zone, close to the DMZ, continued to function and to bring together South Korean companies and Northern workers until 2016. Some private aid continued from the South to the North, and there is a much better understanding of the North in the South. But the high hopes of 2000 faded under conservative governments that ruled from 2008 to 2017. The final blow seemed to come when President Park Geun Hye, Park Chung Hee's daughter, ended South Korean involvement at Kaesong in 2016, in protest at a North Korean missile test. But in 2017 Park's successor, Moon Jae In, moved away from the confrontational policies of his two predecessors. Not all in South Korea were happy at the better relationship with the North, but Moon was determined to work at it.

Visitors to both Koreas will be made aware of the past. War museums and monuments in both countries often feature on tourist programs. Around Seoul, there are many monuments to the UN forces, and to the battles of 1950–51. In both North and South, a tour to the truce village of Panmunjom is a major highlight.

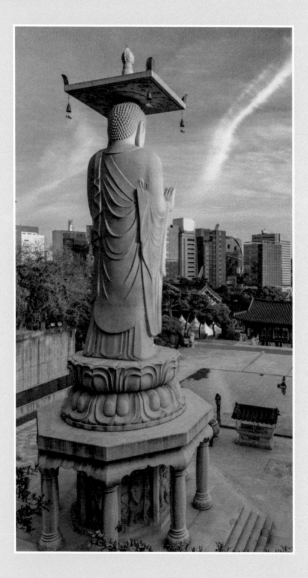

# CHAPTER TWO

# VALUES & ATTITUDES

## SOCIAL RELATIONS

The Chinese long ago described Korea as "the Eastern country of courteous people." This aphorism reflected the Koreans' traditional esteem for decorum, courtesy, and propriety, derived from the teachings of Confucius. Neither North nor South would claim to be Confucian in the traditional manner these days, but Korean hospitality, both North and South, is likely to remain memorable.

Koreans do not favor demonstrative behavior in front of those they do not know well. They tend to be remote and may seem standoffish in the presence of strangers. They are not necessarily friendly toward people they meet on the street, whether Korean or foreign—though the lost-looking foreigner in South Korea will often find somebody willing to help, and foreigners do not get lost in North Korea.

On the whole, Koreans do not feel obliged to greet in a friendly fashion those to whom they have not been introduced. This is very marked in North Korea, where political considerations also come into play. Korean cities are just as impersonal as cities in the West, and all the traditional rules about courtesy go by the board.

In South Korea, the apparent unfriendliness is perhaps more obvious in Seoul or Pusan, but you will see the same behavior in North Korea among a crowd waiting for a bus, for example. Everybody is a stranger, and so people push and shove in a way that they would not do if they felt that they knew those with whom they were mixing. In this respect, the foreign visitor is likely to be treated just like a Korean.

If you can visit a Korean family on their home ground, however, you will meet quite a different reception. There, or in his or her place of work, a Korean will be most courteous and polite to visitors.


## GROUP IDENTITY

Koreans can quickly strike up close relationships when they find that they share something in common with a new acquaintance. Among a group of Koreans, especially when meeting for the first time, great efforts will be made to establish links in common. These can be family, school, or university ties, hometowns shared, or even hobbies. The sense of belonging to a group, of being "one of us," is very important to Koreans and plays a major role in developing human relations. It can also exclude outsiders quite pointedly.

As a foreigner, you will not share family or hometown links, but may have hobbies in common, or possibly, in the case of South Koreans, have attended the same university as your host did when studying in your country. This will provide a useful talking point and social bond. In North Korea you may find, especially among interpreters, people who have read a surprising amount of British and American literature. The peaker of the DPRK parliament, the Supreme People's Assembly, is an admirer of Byron's poetry. This too can provide a bond, although you may also need to spend some time explaining that London is no longer shrouded in a permanent fog, or that things have moved on since Chicago in the 1920s!

It is very likely that you will be asked personal questions about your age, your education, your religion, your marital status—very few Koreans remain unmarried—and the composition of your family. This is neither "nosiness," nor a wish to satisfy idle curiosity, but an attempt to learn important information that will allow your Korean acquaintances to position themselves in relation to you: to be older, married, and with children, or to have a university doctorate, for example, all give social standing.

In South Korea, you may also find that you are questioned closely about your religious beliefs. Again, this has largely to do with establishing common ground—many South Koreans have embraced Western religions and will be seeking a bond between you and them. Be warned, however, that Koreans, like others in

East Asia, differentiate between "Christians," who are from the Protestant tradition, and Catholics, who are not. If you are asked "Are you a Christian?" your interlocutor will almost certainly mean "Are you a Protestant?" Korean Christians may be disappointed if you say "no," but for most Koreans, religion, or the absence of religion, is something personal and they do not probe. Even today, Koreans frequently use "we" when it is more natural in English to say "I." In both North and South, they prefer to say "our country" instead of "my country" and "our house" instead of "my house." You might even hear "our wife" instead of "my wife"! Don't worry. This too is part of the Korean—and indeed wider East Asian—emphasis on the group rather than the individual.

## OLD AND NEW

Some South Koreans at first sight appear very Westernized. The style of life, especially in the cities, is like that found in other big cities throughout the world. War and development have left few ancient buildings. Some modern Korean architecture draws on traditional styles, but most is fairly nondescript. In South Korea, you can eat at McDonalds or Wendy's. Planet Hollywood came to Seoul in the 1980s, as did the Hard Rock Cafe. In addition, there are many Western-style restaurants and shops, run by Koreans, which show the Korean desire to be modern and international. Korean men and women wear Western-style clothes on most occasions.

Korean bride wearing a traditional *hanbok*.

Remember, of course, that "the West" from Korea is not just Europe and the United States, but also includes the Indian subcontinent and the Middle East.

In the North, the number of restaurants used to be very limited and visitors often ended up eating most meals in their hotels. That has changed and now there are many restaurants, especially in Pyongyang. But even outside Pyongyang, there are likely to be at least one or two alternatives to hotel food.

Traditional costume—*hanbok* in the South, *chosun yot* in the North (both mean Korean costume)—is increasingly rare, particularly among men. Just occasionally, a younger South Korean man will appear in traditional dress, especially at New Year's. A few wear it at home and it remains popular among some older men in the South, who may well don it for a Saturday or Sunday outing to the park. There are also some villages in South Korea where traditional costume is generally worn.

North and South Korean women put on traditional dress more frequently than the men, and it is very becoming. You will see women in Korean costume at weddings and the accompanying photographic sessions, in big hotels and traditional restaurants, and at cultural performances, but it is steadily disappearing from everyday life.

## RESPECT FOR ELDERS

One aspect of traditional Korea that has survived is widespread respect for those who are older. This is another inheritance from Confucianism, which is still a strong cultural influence on the Korean peninsula. To show respect to the elderly and to those senior in years is highly regarded. It is therefore not advisable to sit until those more senior have taken their seats, and it also makes a good impression if you stand up when somebody more senior enters the room. You may find that Korean young people are reluctant to eat, drink alcohol, or smoke in front of parents or teachers. If you are young, or even just young-looking, you may find that an older Korean abandons you in mid-conversation to talk to an older colleague. There is little point in taking offense at such actions. No slight is intended to you.

In theory, at least, this respect for seniority extends to those met traveling on buses, trains, and the subway. In practice, however, the anonymity described earlier often takes over, and it is becoming less common for somebody to offer a seat to an elderly person. One vestige of the past that you may still find is for those seated to hold the bags of standing passengers. Do not be surprised, therefore, if a heavy bag is quietly taken from you on buses and trains; it is not a thief but a seated passenger wanting to relieve you of your burden for a few stops. In the North, guides and drivers are likely to be particularly attentive to older people, relieving them of bags even for the shortest distance. You may also find yourself being helped to put on shoes or to get up a hill or a steep staircase.

## ATTITUDES TOWARD WOMEN

Confucius emphasized respect for the elderly, but he meant elderly men. Neither women nor children ranked very high in his (or his followers') system of priorities. In the past, a woman was taught that in youth she should be obedient to her parents; when married, to her husband; and in old age, to her son. Much of this has now changed. Some Korean women will smoke and drink (especially if they are over sixty), lead independent lives, and file for divorce. A growing number manage or own businesses. Women are well represented in some professions. Many are engaged in teaching, and there are numerous female pediatricians. In South Korea, women are now admitted to the military academies for officer training, and the South Korean armed forces have appointed their first female general, although, perhaps true to form, she is a nurse by profession. There is a strong feminist movement in South Korea, with departments specializing in women's studies at several universities. Some women have entered politics, and a few have become ministers. The Minister of Foreign Affairs in 2018 was female, as was the ROK ambassador to London.

In North Korea, women have in theory enjoyed full equality since 1948, and certainly, as in South Korea, women are prominent in professions such as teaching and nursing. Women are also represented in official circles and in the military.

Yet the idea of male superiority and female subordination has not entirely disappeared. A middle-class Korean man, whether North or South, will boast that he is a "tiger" at home, even if he does hand all his wages over to his wife at the end of the month, receiving pocket money in return. Women will show subordination to men, especially in public. Korean women, therefore, are not necessarily used to the courtesies shown to women in the West. They will be pleased if a foreigner holds open a door for them or allows them to go first out of an elevator, though they may also be a little embarrassed at the courtesy and unwilling to accept it at first.

A Western woman in South Korea may find that she is not treated as she would be at home, even if she is conducting business in her own right. Usually the courtesy extended to a visitor will ensure that she is well received during ordinary business transactions— she will be invited to lunch or dinner, especially if this is in a Western restaurant. However, she is unlikely to be included in post-work entertainment, particularly if this is to include a late-night drinking session. In

North Korea, foreign female visitors will probably not find such discrimination, partly because some of the entertainment outlets available in the South do not exist in the North.

## ATTITUDES TOWARD FOREIGNERS

Most Koreans, North and South, are extremely polite to foreigners. If you appear lost, somebody will always try to help. Staff in even the smallest restaurants will do their best to make sure that you eat and drink adequately, even if they have no common language with which to communicate. In conversations or meetings, Koreans will be nonconfrontational and will do everything possible to make foreigners feel at ease.

At the same time, Koreans' past experiences of outside interference in the peninsula's affairs have left some suspicions, which may surface from time to time. While polite to individual Japanese people, and often very attracted to Japanese popular culture and Japanese manufactured goods, Koreans remain very suspicious of the Japanese state and its past record, a suspicion that schools do much to reinforce in their teaching of history. Distrust of the Japanese is at its shrillest in North Korea, but it is not difficult to uncover similar attitudes in the South.

There is also a degree of ambivalence toward China. China is, of course, immensely important in cultural terms, and precolonial Korea tended to look toward China for political support and assistance in times of trouble. At the same time, the Koreans were very conscious that when helping Korea the Chinese were not doing so for altruistic motives, but because what happened in Korea could have repercussions in China. Recent history has added to the ambiguities in this relationship.

For South Korea, after the Communist takeover in China in 1949, and even more after China's intervention in the Korean War, China was a major enemy, allied with North Korea. Since the 1980s, and the establishment of diplomatic relations in 1992, such attitudes have softened, but the memories, and to some extent the suspicions, are still there. In addition, the experience of dealing with the Chinese in recent years has not always been smooth; illegal immigration from China has been a problem, for example. Many dislike China's willingness to return North Korean refugees to an uncertain fate in that country. Others are worried by the growing number of Chinese tourists and their tendency to patronize mainly Chinese-owned establishments. There is also concern in some quarters about growing Chinese economic interests in North Korea, which have much expanded since South Korean companies began to withdraw after 2008. Some fear that China's increasing economic involvement  might lead to more political involvement and the exclusion of South Korea.

North Korea is not entirely happy with its relationship with China. The North Koreans believe that even when the Chinese have come to their assistance, they have put their own interests before those of North Korea. So as far as the North Koreans are concerned, the Chinese did not press for a unified Korea at the 1954 Geneva Conference, preferred to reach an accommodation with the United States in the 1970s rather than advance the cause of world revolution, and, perhaps the greatest betrayal of all, established diplomatic relations with South Korea in 1992. And while the North Koreans are aware that they are heavily dependent on China now that the Soviet Union has disappeared, this has added to their resentment rather than eased it. Many North Koreans think that China only supplies second-rate goods and that, if China's needs demanded it, even the supply of such goods would be reduced or cut off. China's willingness to sign up to international sanctions directed at North Korea and its criticism of the country's missile and nuclear program have put an additional strain on relations. Events in 2018 saw a move away from the hostility that had begun to mark the relationship, but there is always the possibility that it will resurface.

Suspicion of the West exists, too. It is strongest and most obvious in North Korea, where the focus is very much on United States' hostility. Even the food aid that the United States supplied from the late 1990s has not modified hostile feelings toward the superpower. This became more intense after President George W. Bush's reference to North Korea as part of an "axis of evil" in his 2002 State of the Union message. Posters and slogans single out the United States as the principal enemy— though Japan may be shown close behind! Americans who visit North Korea, however, find that this hostility does not extend to them personally. Unfortunately, the tensions between the two countries led to a series of detentions of US citizens, often on what appear trivial charges. The detained included one American student, Otto Wambier, who was only released as he was dying. This led to the US banning its citizens from visiting North Korea in 2017.

In South Korea, too, there is an undercurrent of resentment of the West, again primarily focused on the United States. The United States' presence in the country is very marked, with large numbers of American troops in South Korea since the end of the Korean War. The American bases are large and occupy prime real estate. For many years the main base at Yongsan was in Seoul, right in the heart of the city. The bases have given rise to entertainment districts, prostitution, and all the other features of garrison towns. In such circumstances, resentment seems bound to build up, and it is regularly fueled by incidents involving American forces.

Most of the time, resentment against foreigners remains firmly under the surface, but occasionally it comes out into the open. Late evenings can be a time for caution, as young Korean men go home after an evening's drinking. On the streets or the subway, this is a time to be careful. A foreign man with a Korean woman may come in for verbal abuse and occasionally some form of physical attack, but any foreigner who stands out, or in some way draws attention, may be at risk. Such incidents are rare, but they do happen. It is best to remain calm and to try to move away from the area.

### *Saved by a Korean Granny*

One night, coming back to the hotel from a restaurant some distance behind Seoul's Plaza Hotel with my wife, we became aware of an altercation between a young Korean man and woman, in which the latter seemed to be getting badly hurt. Perhaps fortified by too much *soju*, I shouted out and went to intervene. In one sense this was a successful move, since the young woman was able to escape. In another it was very foolish, since I—middle-aged, with glasses, and very unfit—was now faced by one very angry, fit young man, who turned his attention to me. I remember briefly reflecting that he had probably been taught unarmed combat during military service, which is mandatory for virtually all Korean men.

Rescue was at hand, however. From out of one of the small shops still open, a grandmotherly figure emerged. Perhaps she had been watching, but whatever the reason, she went for the young man and told him in no uncertain terms to go home. Miracle of miracles, he turned away, cursing me as an interfering fool, but departing the scene. The grandmother did not look at us but returned to her vantage point. I was most grateful, but I also learned an important lesson. Avoid interfering in a quarrel between Koreans, even if it is between a man and a woman. You will get no thanks and run the risk of getting badly hurt.

# CHAPTER THREE

# BELIEFS, CUSTOMS, & TABOOS

Over the centuries, Koreans have shown themselves to be adept at assimilating new religious beliefs. Whether it was Buddhism in the fourth century after Christ, or Catholicism in the eighteenth century, Koreans have been quick to take up new doctrines. In the case of Confucianism, which is perhaps more a set of precepts for conducting public and private life than it is a religion, the Koreans so took to it that they would eventually claim to be more correct practitioners than the Chinese, who had developed it in the first place.

## SHAMANISM

A much older religious tradition, shamanism, has survived despite all the new beliefs and all attempts to suppress it. Even today, in the modern city of Seoul, a visitor may come across the *mudang*, or shaman, interceding with the spirit world, and especially with

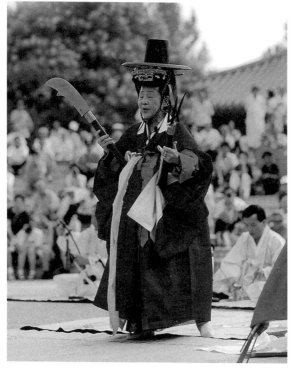

A *mudang* performing a *gut* (ritual) in a state of possession, Seoul.

the dead, on behalf of those on earth. Shamanism is not like other religions in that there is no central authority and no doctrine; rather, each shaman is a self-elected specialist. Most are female. Early Korean kings seem to have had shamanistic roles, and archaeological remains from various early kingdoms include artifacts that appear to be linked with shamanism. The famous gold crowns of Shilla are an example and seem to reflect shamanistic practices in what is now Siberia.

With the arrival of Buddhism (see below), shamanism became marginalized, but it did not disappear. While popular among ordinary people, it also had a following at court during the Koryo period (918–1392). Under the Yi or Chosun dynasty (1392–1910), which was heavily influenced by Confucianism, shamanism was officially excluded from the court. In practice, however, this exclusion was never complete, especially as far as the women of the court were concerned. Shamanism also influenced courtly music and dance, despite the official disapproval. It survived in the Japanese colonial period (1910–45) but was much discriminated against.

Since 1945, shamanism in South Korea has suffered periods of discrimination. After the 1961 military coup, President Park Chung Hee and his military colleagues tried to end shamanistic ceremonies, which they saw as old-fashioned and superstitious. Yet at the same time, "traditional" music was much encouraged, even though it often derived from such rituals. Since Park's assassination in 1979, shamanism has reemerged into a more public position in South Korea. No figures on the number of shamanistic believers in Korea are available. There is nothing in shamanism that prevents its adherents from following other religions as well, and there are strong links between shamanism and Buddhism.

## BUDDHISM

The Maitreya, last of the five earthly buddhas, expected to come in the future.

Buddhism has suffered ups and downs over the centuries but has survived. Introduced from China, according to tradition, from 372 CE onward, it spread from the Koguryo kingdom in the north of the peninsula to the other kingdoms. In turn, Koreans took the new doctrine to Japan. Buddhism had a profound influence both intellectually and as a source of artistic expression. In the Koryo period, Buddhism was both a popular and a court religion. Many monasteries were built, and members of the royal family became monks. Although few monastic buildings from these early periods have survived, statues and other remains testify to the importance of the religion.

Buddhism suffered under the Yi dynasty, with many of the monasteries being suppressed. Under government pressure, the monks were forced out of the cities and new monasteries were built in remote districts; many survive to this day. But anti-Buddhist pressures were not constant, and even some kings who persecuted Buddhism at one stage would turn to it in old age. By the end of the nineteenth century, Buddhism seemed in decline, with many of its ceremonials and rituals almost indistinguishable from shamanism. Visiting foreigners described dirty and ignorant monks, and ramshackle monasteries.

Buddhism did survive, reviving in the face of the growing challenge of Protestant Christianity from the 1880s onward. It also survived what many Koreans saw as a too close relationship with the Japanese authorities, though the divisions then created caused problems within the Buddhist community well into the

Monks after evening worship at Haeinsa Temple.

postliberation period. This was partly because some Buddhists were active in the anti-Japanese movement, even if others worked with the authorities. The Japanese also encouraged Korean monks to marry, as Japanese monks had been doing since the thirteenth century. Today, Korean Buddhism flourishes, with about 10 million, or about a quarter of South Korea's population, claiming to be Buddhists. It has adopted some of Christianity's techniques for involving the faithful, such as collecting funds for welfare, and Buddhists have played a prominent role in opposition to dictatorial rule since 1948. Buddhist nuns have also become active. Korean Buddhism has become better known internationally, especially since a number of monasteries have been willing to accept Westerners as monks since the 1970s.

## CONFUCIANISM

Whether or not Confucianism should be classified as a religion is a long-standing debate. To some, it was, and is, more a social and political philosophy, linked to a series of obligations and ceremonies, than a religious doctrine. Others disagree, seeing in the custom of honoring ancestors, and the honor paid to Confucius in particular, elements of religious practice.

Originally from China, where Confucius lived and taught, Confucianism was well established in Korea by the time of the Three Kingdoms. Its approach to

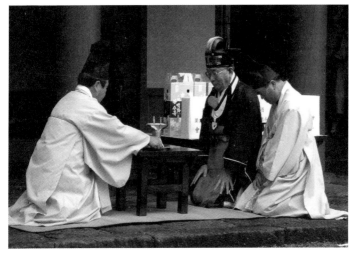

Confucian ritual ceremony in Cheju, South Korea.

the conduct of both public and personal affairs found a welcome acceptance among Koreans. While the more intellectual concepts may not have spread very far in society, the rules of behavior, and especially the honoring of ancestors, seem to have gained a wide acceptance, admittedly encouraged by the state and local authorities. Until the fourteenth century, Confucianism was not dominant—it competed with both shamanism and Buddhism for influence—but it came into its own under the Yi dynasty. The new rulers who took power in the 1390s were anxious to restore relations with China. In doing so, they embraced with enthusiasm Zhu Xi's approach to Confucianism, with its emphasis on rites and obligations, which had become the new orthodoxy in China. Other Confucian principles, such as advancement on the basis of intellectual merit alone, received somewhat less attention, or were modified to suit the Yi dynasty rulers.

Today, few formally claim to be Confucian. Yet the precepts of Confucius still predominate in both Koreas. Respect for elders and respect for authority, both derived from Confucian principles, are strongly ingrained and encouraged. Whether it is students criticizing the government—behavior that many trace back to the idea that the righteous or educated have a duty to tell the truth whatever the consequences—or respect for the Leader, elements of traditional Korean Confucianism continue to come into play.

## CHRISTIANITY

Christianity came to Korea in the eighteenth century. Korean officials visiting Beijing encountered Roman Catholic priests and took back the doctrines of this new religion to Korea. Not only did they study the literature, they also set up a Church of their own. The Roman Catholic hierarchy in China did not approve of this, but it is thus that Korea's involvement with Christianity began.

From the beginning, the state was suspicious of these people who rejected the Confucian rites honoring ancestors and who looked outside the country for spiritual guidance. Thus the persecution of Catholics began almost as soon as the Church was established. It would continue until the 1880s, giving the Korean Church a string of martyrs; more than one hundred of these were canonized in the late twentieth century. One reason for these persecutions was the link between Catholicism and the Western powers; the Korean government's fear of Catholics was intensified by the clear link between Catholic priests and France.

In the 1880s, Protestant Christianity arrived in Korea. American Presbyterians and Methodists predominated. They have left their mark on the puritanical cast of many Korean Church communities, in which the use of alcohol and tobacco is very much frowned upon. These missionaries were followed between 1890 and 1910 by smaller groups such as the Anglicans (Episcopalians) and the Salvation Army. By then the atmosphere had changed and the persecutions ended. Many Koreans welcomed the missionaries as harbingers of the modern world. Protestants would make major contributions to the development of Korean education and social services such as hospitals, as well as having a profound influence in other areas such as music and the spread of the Korean alphabet, *Han'gul*. Christians would play a prominent role in opposition to the Japanese.

Today, South Korea is second only to the Philippines as a center of Christianity in Asia. The total number of Christians, both Catholic and Protestant, is more than 12 million, and growing—as already noted, however, the Koreans, like some others, distinguish between Catholics

Yoido Full Gospel Church on the Han River in the heart of Seoul.

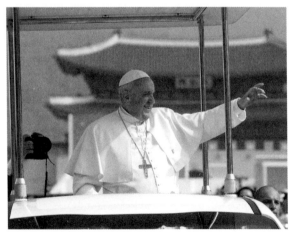

Pope Francis during his visit to South Korea in 2014.

and Christians; the latter term refers to Protestants. Many prominent South Koreans have professed Christianity, including several presidents, and Korean Churches now send missionaries abroad. The Pentecostal Yoido Full Gospel Church claims the largest congregation in the world. Pope John Paul II visited South Korea in 1984 and 1989. Pope Francis visited in August 2014. There is also a small Orthodox community.

## OTHER RELIGIONS AND BELIEFS

A small Muslim community originally developed among Koreans who had moved into northeast China, where they encountered Chinese Muslims, during the Japanese colonial period. Most of these Koreans returned to the peninsula at the end of the war in 1945, but there were no clergy to minister to them. In the 1950s, imams working with the Turkish forces that came to Korea during the Korean War began to minister to these groups and to make additional converts. The first Korean imam was elected in 1955. The conversion of Korean construction workers in the Middle East since the 1960s has boosted the numbers of Korean Muslims since then. Today, the number of Korean Muslims is around the 40,000 mark. The first mosque was erected in Seoul in 1976. There are also mosques in Pusan and some other cities.

In addition to these mainstream religions, Korea has produced several new religions. One, Chondogyo, developed out of the nineteenth-century Tonghak ("Eastern Learning") Rebellion. Today it exists in both North and South Korea, linked to the peasant communities in the countryside. Probably the best known outside Korea is the Unification Church, often called the "Moonies" after its founder, the Reverend Moon Sun Myong (1916–2012). Moon, born in what is now North Korea, was originally a Presbyterian minister, but his Church now is far removed from orthodox Christianity. While it has attracted a considerable following outside Korea, the number of its Korean adherents is relatively small. In South Korea it has many business interests, and although Moon was for long seen as anti-Communist, he began visiting North Korea in the 1980s. He met Kim Il Sung on several of his visits. When he died in 2012, Kim Jung Un sent a wreath and he was posthumously awarded a DPRK decoration. The Unification Church has business interests in North Korea, including an involvement with the Potonggang Hotel and a joint venture automobile factory near Pyongyang. The Church has sometimes been favored by the South Korean authorities and sometimes restricted.

The South Korean religious scene today is a vibrant one. The visitor cannot fail to be reminded of this in any Korean town or city, where neon-lit crosses can be seen in abundance at night. Many Koreans remain eclectic in their religious beliefs; just because a person professes one set of beliefs does not mean that he or she will not be interested in, or even participate in, the activities of other religious groups. This causes no problems with Buddhism and shamanism, or even Confucianism, but Christianity, whether Catholic or Protestant, has tried, not always successfully, to be more exclusive.

As well as religious believers, South Korea has a sizeable minority of people who profess no religion. Census returns show that some 15 percent of the population claim that they are atheists.

## RELIGION IN THE NORTH

It is not easy to write with certainty about religion in North Korea. Before 1945, the northern half of the peninsula had many Buddhist temples and hermitages, and the same religious mix prevailed as elsewhere on the peninsula. With the arrival of Christianity, the north proved fertile ground for missionary work. Since it was closer to China, new ideas often came into the northern areas first. By 1910, Pyongyang, where several Protestant missionary groups had their headquarters, was regarded as a major Christian city throughout Asia. Pyongyang Foreign School was the school of choice for missionary families in China and Japan as well as those in Korea. Among its graduates is Ruth Graham, who married the celebrated American evangelist, Billy Graham. Kim Il Sung, North Korea's leader, came from a family that had Christian connections, and his mother seems to have been a believer. He admitted attending church but wrote in his autobiography that he found it boring.

With the Soviet occupation of the north after 1945, and the establishment of the DPRK in 1948, all that ended. Religion was not proscribed; freedom of religion officially existed, and both the Soviet forces and the new North Korean state tried to make use of some prominent religious leaders to add to their legitimacy. But faith was subject to tight control, and the official line of the Korean Workers' Party, like that of other Communist parties, was that religion was the "opium of the people"—nothing but superstition that had done much harm in the past. Many clergy and believers fled to South Korea, a trend that intensified during the Korean War. During the war, churches and temples were destroyed along with most other substantial buildings.

From the armistice until the late 1970s, the North Korean authorities made no attempt to rebuild religious centers. A few Buddhist monasteries survived as historical monuments rather than centers of religion. What appeared to be token religious bodies existed, but they were not much in evidence. From South Korea came persistent claims that religious believers in the North were subject to intense persecution.

The 1980s saw a change. Visitors to Buddhist temples found that people calling themselves monks now once again occupied them. A Roman Catholic church and two Protestant churches were built in

Pyongyang, one close to the site both of Kim Il Sung's mother's birthplace and of the church at which she used to worship. A Chondogyo temple also appeared. The religious bodies, long inactive, began to function. The explanation given was that previously the state had lacked funds with which to reconstruct churches and temples destroyed during the Korean War. Now it could afford to do so. It is also sometimes claimed that the lack of such buildings had not hindered those who wished to do so from following their religious practices; they had met in houses or on the sites of former religious buildings.

Since then, many foreigners and South Koreans have visited the churches and temples. Billy Graham preached at the Bongsu Church, while the Vatican maintains a link with the Catholic Church in Pyongyang. In 2003, after North Korea's late leader, Kim Jong Il, had visited Russia, he arranged for a Russian Orthodox Church to be built in Pyongyang, and there are, apparently, worshipers. Whether these are manifestations of real religious belief, or, as some allege, merely actors going through the motions for the benefit of gullible outsiders, nobody knows. North Korean exiles regularly allege that true believers still suffer savage persecution.

It is believed that there are some Muslims in North Korea, descended from *hui*, or Chinese Muslims. The only known mosque is at the Iranian Embassy, built c. 2012, which apparently hosts both Shiite and Sunni Muslims from among diplomats and aid workers.

## CUSTOMS

Korea's rich religious inheritance has affected its customs and traditions. Whatever their religion, most Koreans observe some form of Confucian ceremony to mark auspicious occasions, even if they do not realize that what they are doing is of Confucian origin. These include the celebration of one hundred days after a baby's birth—a child that had survived so long was likely to live—and the celebration of the sixtieth birthday. Many Korean marriages reflect some aspects of the Christian wedding ceremony, even if it is only in the wearing of a white wedding dress. In South Korea,

Float for the Buddha's birthday parade in Daegu, South Korea.

believers and nonbelievers alike incorporate Christmas and Buddha's birthday into their informal calendar, and even in the North these dates do not go wholly unnoticed. North and South, shamanistic sounds and costumes linger on in what have come to be called farmers' bands.

Traditionally, the main festivals of the year began with the Lunar (sometimes called "Chinese" in the West) New Year, which falls from late January to late February. This was, and is, a time for dressing up, family visits, and feasting. Although both North and South Korea tried to substitute January 1, and in both that day is still an official holiday and the start of the

The festival of Daeboreum, or "Great Full Moon," ushers in the Lunar New Year.

year, both have accepted that the pull of the Lunar New Year is too strong, and it is now a holiday period throughout the peninsula.

The other great traditional festival was Chusok, the fall harvest festival, a time for returning home if possible, honoring one's ancestors, cleaning graves,

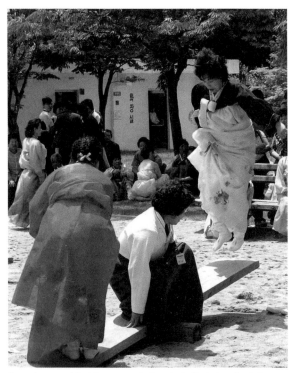

Seesawing, part of the folk games at the Dano festival in Andong, South Korea.

Rooted in village life, Pungmul performances include drumming, dancing, and singing.

and celebrating the new crops. In South Korea, it is nowadays an occasion for some of the most spectacular traffic jams and crowded planes and trains, as everybody who is able struggles to get home. In North Korea, where travel is more difficult, few people return home—though if they can, they do. Instead families picnic in the parks or beside rivers, and, in the more relaxed atmosphere of recent years, once again display pictures of deceased family members. They may also bring the ashes of cremated family members along to the picnic.

Some of the main public holidays in the two Koreas are shown overleaf.

## SOUTH KOREA

**January 1**  New Year's Day

**Late January–late February**  Lunar New Year

**March 1**  Independence Movement Day

**April 5**  Arbor Day

**May 5**  Children's Day

**8th day of 4th lunar month**  Buddha's birthday

**June 6**  Memorial Day

**July 17**  Constitution Day

**August 15**  Liberation Day

**15th day of 8th lunar month**  Chusok

**October 3**  National Foundation Day

**December 25**  Christmas Day

## NORTH KOREA

**January 1**  New Year

**Late January–late February**  Lunar New Year

**February 16**  Kim Jong Il's birthday

**April 15**  Kim Il Sung's birthday

**April 25**  Army Day

**May 1**  May Day

**July 27**  Victory Day

**August 15**  Liberation Day

**September 9**  Founding of the DPRK

**15th day of 8th lunar month**  Chusok

**October 10**  Founding of the Korean Workers' Party

**December 27**  Socialist Constitution

## TABOOS

All countries have taboos, and the Koreas are no exception. Traditionally, white clothes rather than black were worn for mourning, but this was a special type of white cloth, an off-white hemp rarely seen except at funerals today. A white mourning band is still common, but a black band is also often worn nowadays for mourning purposes. You are in any case unlikely to be invited to a funeral, but you might find yourself expected to pay respects if somebody of your acquaintance happens to die while you are in the country. Usually this will involve attending a memorial hall and solemnly bowing in front of a picture of the deceased.

Many Koreans, like Chinese, still avoid the number four (*sa*) since it has the same pronunciation as the word for death. You will often find that some Korean buildings will not have a fourth floor, or that the letter "F" replaces the number four. Because many Koreans are aware of Western superstitions about the number thirteen, that too may be missing.

Another common taboo is against the use of the left hand to offer an object to somebody. To use the left hand is seen by all Koreans as offensive. It is best to offer something to another person, especially if they are senior in age or rank to you, with both hands. If that is not possible, use the right hand.

Do not stick chopsticks upright in rice, as this resembles the way incense is burned at funerals.

Bare feet are generally to be avoided. Koreans live, eat, and sleep on the floor, so it is important that floors are spotlessly clean. Not wearing socks means that your feet will be dirty. (I have been reprimanded for not wearing socks with sandals by a total stranger on the streets of Seoul!)

If you find that your host is diffident about some issue, do not push too hard. Sometimes a slightly diffident attitude hides a real problem, and if you pursue the issue too much, your host or counterpart will feel a loss of face. Similarly, try not to lose your temper, however much you may feel provoked—you may not feel embarrassed, but your host will.

All gifts should be wrapped, no longer necessarily in particular colors. However, avoid using red pens when writing notes, addressing mail, or signing a letter or document.

Do not touch an adult on the head, or even the shoulder. The same prohibition does not apply to children or youngsters, but it is best to err on the side of caution and avoid touching any Korean on the head.

Until recently, homosexuality was very rarely acknowledged in South Korea—and it is still not acknowledged in the North. Today its existence is more widely accepted in the South, especially among university students, but you may still find Koreans who argue that it is something only known in the West. Do not assume that two boys or two girls walking hand in hand are homosexual. Walking thus, or with arms about each other's shoulders, is not a taboo in Korea, merely a sign of friendship. Conversely, a man and a woman who show too much affection in public will attract disapproval.

There are few formal restrictions on photography in South Korea nowadays. Some older people, especially in the countryside, may object to having their photograph taken, and it is best to avoid giving offense. As in many other countries, it is wise not to photograph anything that looks like a military installation or could be for military purposes. This may include airports. One should also be careful at Panmunjom, the village in the Demilitarized Zone separating the two Koreas.

Restrictions on photography in North Korea are likely to be more irksome. The North Koreans have become very sensitive about visitors abusing their position as guests to take what are seen as hostile photographs—that is, they show the country in a bad light. If you see any sign of hostility, abandon the effort. And of course, avoid any military object, including soldiers, and airports. Control of photography at Pyongyang's Sunan Airport appears to be less stringent than in the past but taking pictures there could still get visitors into trouble. Digital cameras have made it easier to check what pictures you have taken, and some people have been forced to delete photographs deemed offensive.

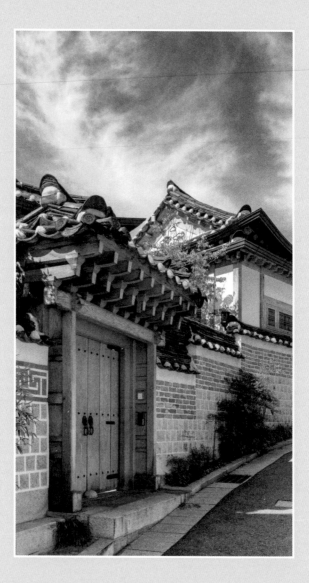

# CHAPTER FOUR

# THE KOREANS AT HOME

There are major differences between home life in South and North Korea. It is not impossible to visit a North Korean house or apartment, but it is rare, and to many people most such visits feel contrived. Clearly, one is shown only the best and it is impossible to tell how typical the dwellings are. If you are entertained in North Korea, it will be in a restaurant, at one of the many guest houses in Pyongyang, or in a hotel either in the capital or in the provinces. If your business takes you into the countryside, you might be lucky enough to be entertained at lunch or dinner on a collective farm. The best local produce will appear, and there will be much jolly drinking—though some of the liquors produced on such occasions may take a bit of getting used to!

So, most people who meet Koreans at home will meet South Koreans. Unlike the Japanese, Koreans do seem to enjoy entertaining at home; this is partly because Korean houses or apartments are generally larger than those available to the Japanese, especially in the cities.

## HOUSING

Most Koreans today live in cities; a quarter of the country's population live in Seoul. In Seoul especially, the favored accommodation consists of high-rise apartment blocks. These blocks, which began to appear in the 1960s, are now all over the city, and they carry none of the negative associations that such buildings have acquired in some Western European countries. To Koreans, the tower blocks represent Manhattan or downtown Chicago, rather than the discredited housing estates of London's East End or the suburbs of Paris. The blocks are safe, with guards, and guaranteed utility

Pedestrianized stretch of Sejong-ro avenue in downtown Seoul.

supplies and parking spaces. This is the epitome of middle-class living, and most South Koreans think of themselves as middle class.

Inside, some attempt at reconstructing aspects of a traditional Korean house takes place. Shoes are not worn, for example, and there may be some rooms in which the family live at floor level; the older members of the family may still prefer to sleep on the floor, while younger people may use Western-style beds. The balcony, if there is one, might have *kimchi* jars on it in winter, as Korean housewives often still prefer to make their own winter *kimchi* (pickled cabbage; see pages 97–9). But there will also be a Western-style sitting room, complete with up-to-date electronic equipment. The furniture will probably be quite heavy in style.

## INVITATIONS HOME

If you are being entertained, you will almost certainly start off in the sitting room, with pre-lunch or dinner drinks and snacks. The latter may well be a mixture of East and West, so expect dried squid as well as Pringles. The meal, however, will almost certainly be Korean food, and may well be eaten in traditional style, seated on the floor. Very few Koreans serve Western food at home even if they eat it outside; most Koreans find Western food rather bland, without the bite of the spices used in traditional Korean dishes. Drinks served with the meal, however, will probably include beer or wine rather than traditional Korean drinks. Koreans tend not to eat heavy sweets as a dessert, preferring a platter of various fruits. Some may offer tea or coffee, but many will not. As with meals in restaurants, once the meal is over it is usual to leave fairly promptly.

As in the West, if invited to a house it is polite to bring a gift. Flowers are acceptable, as is Western liquor. The former can be bought at one of the many flower stalls in Seoul, which will prepare them in suitable fashion; the latter should be from the upper end of the market and be gift-wrapped. A book about your country—or your own book, if you have one—is also a good gift idea. Wedgwood ware and similar products also make acceptable gifts, as do Western-style teas.

Most topics can be discussed on such visits. In the past, politics could be difficult, but the major changes in the political scene since the election of Kim Young Sam as president in 1992 have meant that few subjects are now taboo. If you have been to North Korea, you may well find that your hosts have many questions. The North is still little known in the South, and people are anxious for information. Be warned, however, that many South Koreans remain suspicious of the North, and such attitudes are reinforced at school and during military service. It is probably wise not to appear too enthusiastic on this particular subject.

Even in a social context, many older Koreans will appear somewhat formal. Here, again, Confucian influences come into play; a degree of formality in language and behavior is regarded as the proper course, especially for a senior figure in business, politics, or education. Similarly, formality in dress is the rule, unless you are told otherwise. Do not be fooled by professions of informality; err on the side of a sober style of dress and you cannot go wrong.

## EDUCATION

Koreans both North and South attach high importance to education, and they have some of the highest literacy rates in the world. This is partly because the Korean alphabet is so simple to learn and sticks to simple principles. Also important is the very high premium

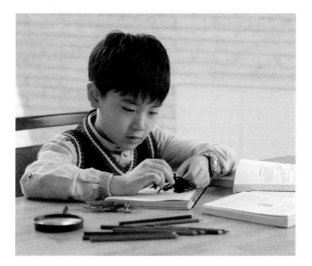

that traditional Korean society placed on education. Education—especially the study of the Confucian classics—was the means of advancement. It opened the doors to government office and thus to worldly success. In the last years of the Korean kingdom and under the Japanese (1910–45), education changed to a more modern curriculum, but few Koreans were able to go beyond the high school level. After independence, both Koreas worked hard to reduce the high illiteracy rates that had prevailed under the Japanese. Today it is almost impossible to find a Korean who cannot read and write. In addition, a massive expansion of educational outlets at all levels began after 1945 and continues today.

The Seoul campus of Kyung Hee University, a private university in South Korea.

## University Education

Korea's modern higher education system began in the late nineteenth century with the establishment of missionary schools. A number of these later became colleges and eventually universities. Under the Japanese, a system of state-run universities began, but these were for Japanese people living in Korea rather than for Koreans. Only after 1945 did such institutions become generally available to young Koreans.

Today South Korea has a widespread net of state universities, with Seoul National University (SNU) at the apex of the system. Private universities also flourish, including many whose reputation ranks with SNU and which also enjoy international acclaim. They include Ewha (a women's college) and Yonsei University, both missionary colleges. Some are highly specialized, others more general. Altogether there are more than 200 four-year colleges, with nearly 2 million students in South Korea. Many universities run courses for non-Korean students, with an increasing use of English for teaching purposes. The courses range from short-term training in Korean to full-scale degrees. About 90,000 foreign students are enrolled in South Korean universities, at all levels from undergraduate to Ph.D. Many South Korean students study abroad, especially in the United States.

North Korea's main center for higher education is Kim Il Sung University, founded in 1946. Young North Koreans eagerly compete for places at this establishment, whose graduates fill many of the top positions in the country. Also popular is Pyongyang University of Foreign Studies. Other colleges exist in Pyongyang and throughout the rest of the country. Foreigners have attended language courses in Pyongyang's universities, and in the past North Korea trained some foreign students in other disciplines. Since 2011, a foreign-run university, the Pyongyang University of Science and Technology, has existed just outside Pyongyang. It has many foreign teachers and links to South Korean and foreign universities. A few foreign universities have begun to establish links with North Korean universities, but such relationships are complicated at present by the extensive international sanctions that apply because of the North's nuclear and missile programs.

## International Schools

Seoul Foreign School, founded in 1912 for the children of missionaries, is the oldest international school in Korea. Since the 1980s it has also had a British School associated with it. There are several other international schools in Seoul, and a few in other cities, including Pusan, Taegu, and Ulsan. French, German, Chinese, and Japanese schools also exist. Foreign schools and universities have begun to set up branches in South Korea. Seoul, Inch'on, and Cheju are popular sites for these establishments.

Before 1941, Pyongyang Foreign School, also founded by missionaries, was one of the main international schools in Asia. It has long since disappeared, but in the 1980s a small Korean-run "International School" for resident foreign children opened in Pyongyang, the only such school in North Korea.

## FRIENDSHIP

Koreans rarely refer to somebody as a "friend" unless they know that person quite well. "Friend" in Korean conveys the idea of what is signified by "close friend" in English. Perhaps more than in the West, there is a distinction in Korea between friends and acquaintances. In Korea, "friendship" involves obligations. Most Koreans therefore will have only a handful of friends, often acquired in school and college days, or, among men, while doing national service. These friendships and links last. That said, it is wholly possible for a foreigner to make real friends in Korea, and well worth the effort; however, a deep level of commitment is expected, and this may sometimes seem like an encroachment on one's hospitality.

Note that in North Korea, as in China, there is often great play made with the title "old friend." This tends to mean a person who has visited the country more than once, and who has displayed a friendly attitude. "Old friends" are deemed to have indicated a degree of sincerity in their interactions that entitles them to special treatment.

### True Friends

Koreans believe that if you are friends, you go along with your friends' wishes, however inconvenient these might be. We found this out one Christmas Day in Seoul, when we had a variety of colleagues from the Embassy over for lunch and then for the evening. Unexpectedly, a Korean colleague telephoned to say that he would be bringing around a group of Koreans to discuss a planned academic seminar to be held early in the New Year. Protests were to no avail, and the group arrived in mid-afternoon. Seemingly nonplussed by our festive hats and clearly merry condition, they stayed for several hours, insisting on discussing the arrangements for the seminar while mince pies and brandy flowed all around. True friends are accepting …

## NAMES

The most common Korean surnames are Kim, Lee, and Park, in that order. (You will also find the surname "Lee" romanized as "Rhee," "Ri," "Yi," "Li," and "I," although in the Korean script these are all spelled the same way. "Park," strictly speaking, should be romanized as "Pak," but most Koreans seem to think that "Park" is a better guide to the sound.) As a result, millions of Koreans share the same surname although they may not be related. Families distinguish themselves by their place of origin, such as "Andong." Thus, you will find that the "Andong Kims" are a family whose clan shrine is in Andong. Most surnames are one syllable, though there are a few two-syllable ones; "SaKong" is one example.

Given names are very important in distinguishing people. Most Koreans have two-syllable given names. Frequently, the family members of one sex in one generation will share one of the syllables. The former North Korean leader, Kim Jong Il, named his three sons Kim Jong Nam, Kim Jong Chul, and Kim Jong Un. In the past, Koreans rarely used their given names. In childhood, their parents would use somewhat jocular and insulting names, designed to prevent evil spirits recognizing and damaging the child. The then North Korean leader, Kim Jong Il, was referring to this custom when he referred to his lack of height in deprecatory terms to the then US Secretary of State, Madeleine Albright, in 2000. It is still regarded as impolite to use an adult's given name, and even Korean students will address each other by their surnames, or as brother and sister. The English terms "Mr.," "Mrs.," and "Miss" are often used by younger Koreans. Older Koreans will prefer official titles, such as chairman, president, professor, or teacher, especially in situations where Westerners might have moved on to a given name basis.

Koreans who have lived abroad, or who have spent a lot of time with foreigners, may be more relaxed about the use of given names. This is especially true of Koreans who have adopted a Western name while abroad, which they can use when they are among foreigners. It is always sensible to check, however, that a Korean acquaintance is willing to be addressed by his or her given name in Korea.

Also note that Korean women retain their own surnames after marriage. Do not be surprised, therefore, if Mr. Kim introduces his wife as Mrs. Park. Some Koreans who have spent a long time in the West may have assimilated the Western practice regarding a wife's name, but it is best not to assume that this is the case.

In the North, there is widespread use of the title "Madame" to refer to married women. Diplomats wives are invariably referred to as "Mr. X's Madame." One gets used to it.

## ACCEPTABLE CONDUCT

Although younger Korean couples may now be seen holding hands in city streets, even in North Korea, older

Koreans generally tend not to show affection in public, except to small children. They will not be offended by foreigners exchanging a brief hug or kiss on greeting but will be surprised if this is repeated frequently. You should also avoid expressions of displeasure. Displays of bad temper are regarded as the height of bad manners and are unlikely to achieve much. It is also best to avoid direct criticism as far as possible. If you have to criticize, do it in a vague and roundabout way, and do not do it in public. The direct approach will leave your audience embarrassed and uncooperative.

Koreans may slurp soup, burp after a meal, and clear their throats noisily, but they do not blow their noses in public. If you have to, always turn your head away from the person you are interacting with. Being considerate and discreet is the rule of thumb for any conduct you are unsure of. In general, be guided in such matters by how your Korean companions are behaving. You are not obliged to burp if you do not wish to, still less to clear throat energetically! You will notice that Koreans who have colds will often wear a surgical mask over their mouths and noses.

Many Korean men, North and South, smoke quite heavily, and although restrictions are beginning to arise in both Koreas, smoking is rarely prohibited in restaurants and other public places. Foreign brands of cigarettes are available but expensive. Younger Korean women rarely smoke, at least in public, but older ones, especially countrywomen, frequently do.

# CHAPTER FIVE

# FOOD & DRINK

## KOREAN CUISINE

The staple food of Korea is short-grain rice, which in the past was sometimes blended with other grains to stretch limited supplies. It is eaten from a ceramic or metal rice bowl with or without a lid. Other tableware includes a soup bowl and various small and large plates for a variety of other foods, often called side dishes. Food is eaten with a metal spoon and a pair of metal chopsticks. Although elsewhere in Asia you will sometimes come across silver chopsticks, the everyday use of metal ones seems to be a uniquely Korean characteristic.

Sometimes you will be given wooden chopsticks in a restaurant. Unlike the Japanese and the Chinese, who use chopsticks for eating rice, the Koreans use a spoon. It is thought to be somewhat gauche to use chopsticks for rice, and under no circumstances stick your chopsticks upright in your rice. Try to master the use of chopsticks and spoon as a courtesy to your hosts

Rice cakes made with steamed flour.

and for your own convenience. In some restaurants, no other implements will be available. The food comes already cut into bite-size pieces, and a knife in particular is considered a coarse object to bring to the table.

Koreans eat three full meals a day, with the number of dishes increasing at each meal. Traditionally, rice, soup, and *kimchi* (see below) appeared at all three meals, which meant that Korean housewives had to be up early to get everything ready before the rest of the family came to the table. Nowadays, many younger South Koreans in the cities have turned to Western-style cereals or toast as an alternative breakfast.

In the past, food was served not in staged courses but all at once and eaten together. This was true in restaurants as well as private homes until recently.

Before the 1986 Asian Games in Seoul, the South Korean government decided that this was wasteful and not suitable for foreigners—who were not consulted—and decreed that all food should be served as separate courses, ordered individually. Gradually, however, the traditional way is creeping back. It is, in fact, easier for a foreigner to order a complete meal than to sort out the complexities of a Korean à la carte menu.

You are not expected to consume everything that is put in front of you, but try as many dishes as you wish. Koreans consider it indelicate to lift the bowl of soup or rice to the lips as is done in China and Japan, or to use one's hands to pick up food. In a traditional restaurant and in many homes, food will be served on low, individual lacquered tables, with each diner having a complete meal on his or her table. Diners sit on cushions on the floor.

### Kimchi

The most famous of all Korean side dishes is *kimchi*. There are many forms of this dish, but the best known is made up of pickled cabbage seasoned with red pepper, garlic, ginger, and shrimp brine (a source of probiotics as *kimchi* ferments over time). Winter *kimchi* was traditionally made in the fall to last the whole winter and was often the only source of vitamin C from November to March. Scientific studies have shown that, while the level of vitamin C in *kimchi* declines as the winter progresses, it really does last until March if properly made in November.

Winter *kimchi* is still made, even in urban households, although today there are many other sources of vitamin C available and it is possible to buy *kimchi* in supermarkets. Its pungent taste and smell can be quite a shock. In the summer, you will find mild "water *kimchi*," usually made from cucumbers in a light brine. There are more than twenty regional variations of *kimchi*, each seasoned in different ways. Some caution is recommended when you first try it, but most people come to like it. Foreigners find that some *kimchi* goes well with Western dishes; roast lamb seems to benefit from the strong flavor. *Kimchi* is such an important part of most Koreans' diet that you should not be surprised if it is served with Chinese and Japanese food in Korea.

*Kimchi* in North Korea is less rich than in the South, though there are many local variations. Everybody will

Jars used for fermenting *kimchi*.

*Oi-sobagi*, or cucumber *kimchi*.

have their own preferences, but we found that the best *kimchi* we ate in North Korea was that available around Kaesong, on the dividing line with the South.

## Popular Dishes

These include *bulgogi*, or "Korean barbecue" as it is sometimes known. Strips of beef are marinated in sesame oil, soy sauce, garlic, ginger, and other condiments, and then cooked over a charcoal or gas brazier at the table. Short ribs, *kalbi*, are also popular and are cooked in the same way. Koreans eat much fish and seafood. As in Japan, raw fish, served with piquant seasonings, is highly regarded. Many styles of soup are served.

Two dishes formerly exclusive to the royal court now often appear at special banquets. The first is *kujolpan*,

*Bulgogi, soju,* and *Nakji bokkeum,* fried, marinaded octopus and vegetables.

often called, somewhat poetically, "nine treasure dish."
This consists of small pancakes and eight special dishes,
all presented in a nine-compartment lacquer dish.
You select a pancake and one or more of the other
dishes, wrap the latter in the former, and away you go.
The second is *sinsullo,* an individual hotpot with beef,
vegetables, and a variety of other ingredients all cooked
over live coals—very hot and very delicious. You
will find that the various ways of preparing food are
similar in North and South Korea, though again, some
traditional regional variations are evident.

Garlic forms an important part of the Korean diet.
It is widely used both on its own and as part of other
dishes. Raw cloves of garlic will often appear as a side
dish, or for adding to dishes such as *bulgogi* as they

*Sinsullo*, royal casserole.

are cooking. Small dishes of pickled garlic are also likely to appear on the table. There is no obligation to eat this, except on the principle of "if you can't beat them, join them." After a time, most people get used to the all-pervasive scent of garlic and fail to notice it.

Some hostile publicity in recent years has focused on the eating of dog meat and on what are described as other "strange foods" in Korea. Some Koreans do eat dog, usually in the form of a soup called *poshintang*, or "body strengthening soup," but it is most unlikely that this would be offered to a foreigner. The dogs, they point out, are not family pets, but are species bred for the table, just like cattle or pigs, and as the same ethics apply they find the singling out of this custom by foreigners offensive and unnecessary.

In South Korea, dog restaurants and those selling other exotic foods unfamiliar to foreigners were subject to strict regulation during the lead-up to the 1988 Olympics, but the controls have generally been relaxed since then. Few foreigners are likely to be aware of their existence and they will make no attempt to attract foreign customers. In 2018, it was announced that the Seoul city authorities had closed down the main complex of dog slaughterhouses serving the city, and the custom may well be on the way out.

Less likely to be offensive, but certainly unusual to Western palates, are the numerous wild plants that Koreans eat. These include certain types of bracken, acorns made into a jelly, and bellflower roots. They are often pickled, or served in light brine, and most foreigners who are prepared to try them find that they are quite tasty, and they may even come to like them.

Meals will usually end with plain fruit. In a restaurant, you will often be brought a towel—hot in winter, cold in summer—to wipe your hands on before the meal, and another at the end.

A growing number of Western-style restaurants can be found in Korean cities. In the past, most of these were in the big hotels, but this is no longer necessarily the case. All styles of food can be found, from the ubiquitous hamburger to the most up-to-date French and Italian cooking. Seoul had a Pakistani restaurant in the early 1980s, and now has several Indian restaurants.

There are also many Chinese and Japanese restaurants, at prices to suit all pockets. Many are very good indeed. In the provinces, the variety of food will be smaller, except in big cities such as Pusan or Taegu. While it may be possible to eat Japanese or Chinese food, both might be heavily "Koreanized." Western food may be limited to steak, or to the widely available "surf and turf"—giant prawns and steak, a dish that has come to Korea via Japan.

In recent years, "fusion food," combining different traditions in one meal, has become increasingly widespread, and restaurants serving this style of food are now common in Seoul, though less so elsewhere. It is also increasingly likely to feature in formal banquets in both Koreas.

In North Korea, there are many restaurants available to foreigners in Pyongyang. They include a number of Japanese-style restaurants, an excellent Cantonese restaurant at the Yanggakdo Hotel, and a good Japanese-derived Western-style restaurant at the Potonggang Hotel. The latter also has had in the past a good selection of foreign wines, including a magnificent Chablis—though at horrific prices! Most restaurants, naturally, serve Korean food, but a surprising number can also provide a selection of Japanese, Chinese, and Western dishes—the last firmly in the Russian tradition, although this is changing. Outside Pyongyang, the choice is more limited, but visitors are often surprised at just what is on offer.

## DRINKING

Koreans like drinking alcohol, and there is little social stigma attached to getting drunk, at least as far as men are concerned. Women may find that their Korean counterparts, especially older women, do not drink much alcohol, although there are exceptions. Drinking parties, especially among men, are common and very popular. Younger people, especially students, will now drink in mixed groups. A few drinks shared in a bar with Korean acquaintances will go a long way toward establishing friendships. Koreans do not as a rule drink alone, and they do not drink much without eating fairly substantial snacks called *anju*. This does not stop them getting drunk, however, and drinking parties may often become quite boisterous. Such sessions may be used to let off steam and to criticize

Cheese and tuna rice rolls wrapped in *gim*, a sheet of dried seaweed.

the boss to his face, but without the dire consequences this might have in the West. The convention is that remarks made at drinking parties are not referred to the next day.

When drinking, even in an informal setting, you should not pour your own drinks. You should hold your glass in front of you, with both hands or with the right hand supported under the elbow by the left hand, and allow somebody else to pour for you. Similarly, you should offer to fill other people's glasses in the same way. If a person toasts you, they will probably drain their glass. You should do the same, at least on the first occasion. During a toast, keep the rim of your glass lower than that of other people's glasses if they are older than you, especially in a formal setting.

At more formal functions, Western-style wine may be available in both North and South, as well as some form of spirit-based drink. The quality of wine will vary a lot. In South Korea, there is a small domestic wine industry, producing mainly German-style white wines, but good quality foreign wines are also available at a price. In North Korea, the choice is more limited, and some very bad wine has been around in the past. In recent years, more drinkable wines, including wines from Latin America and Australia, have appeared in shops catering to foreigners. These may sometimes appear at formal occasions.

Beer is very popular in South Korea. There are several well-known Korean brands, including OB, Hite, and Cass. Most Korean beer is German-style lager, but dark beers can be found. Foreign brands, usually brewed in Korea under license, are also widely available in the big cities, at a price. Heineken, Budweiser, and Carlsberg are popular foreign brands. Some hotels offer even more exotic foreign beers, including both Guinness and British-style draft beer.

As mentioned above, Western-style wine is made in South Korea. The white tends to be better than the red. As one friend put it, "the whites are young, but the reds are positively infantile!" Things are improving slowly. French, Italian, American, and Australian wines can be found in restaurants, and are often now on sale in hotel shops, in both the big department stores and smaller supermarkets and convenience stores, and, in Seoul and some other cities, in specialist wine shops. Whiskey and gin, both imported and locally produced, are widely available. Foreign brands are expensive, especially in hotels, where they are best avoided. Johnny Walker Black Label and Chivas Regal are particularly well-known brand names among Koreans, and they make good presents.

Traditional Korean alcoholic drinks are enjoying something of a revival in both Koreas. They are worth sampling if you get the chance. The most common ones are *soju*, the cheapest, generally the strongest, and rather like vodka, though often only about 25 percent alcohol by volume; *makkoli*, a milky-white drink, sometimes compared to beer; and *chong-jong*, a rice wine, similar to Japanese saké and, like saké, usually served hot, although it is common nowadays to find it served cold in summer. *Popchu*, a higher-quality saké-like drink available in the South, is well worth seeking out.

Much of the above also applies to North Korea. Scotch whiskey is popular, especially but not exclusively among those who have traveled or lived abroad. Even remote hotels are likely to come up with a bottle or two of Scotch. Beer is widely available, much of it made locally. In Pyongyang, there are microbreweries in hotels and restaurants. The acquisition of a former Ushers' brewery from England, together with German techniques, has led to a much improved quality of bottled beer in the capital at least. Foreign beers, especially from Japan or China, are often available. *Soju* is readily available, as are fruit-based liqueurs. Western-style wines, usually from Latin America, can also be found in supermarkets and other shops catering to foreigners.

In the past, Korean women did not drink until they were over sixty. Today, it is not unusual for a Korean woman to take a glass of wine at dinner, though most still stick to orange juice. A few will drink quite a lot. However, women rarely get drunk—it is bad form for them to do so—and a Western woman will need to take this into account. In any case, as we have seen, a Western woman is unlikely to be invited to the more riotous parties. Although Korean men and women traditionally socialize mainly with their own sex, they generally understand Westerners' expectations of a mixed social gathering.

If you do not drink, do not worry. There are many Koreans who do not drink alcohol. Many "Christians" do not touch alcohol. It is also well understood that those taking certain medicines should avoid alcohol. More recently, random breath tests by the police have persuaded many South Koreans not to drink and drive. So if you wish to be excused, you can plead that you have religious convictions, that you are taking medication, or that you are driving.

## TOASTS

At formal meals, the custom of toasting is very popular. Formal toasts and formal speeches, if there are to be any, may well take place at the beginning of the meal, before any eating has begun. On such occasions, the principal host and the principal guest will normally propose and respond to the toasts. You should note that while it is usual to drink beer, wine, and soft drinks as you wish, the spirit glass is normally reserved for drinking toasts. Often this will be Scotch whiskey, though traditional Korean spirits such as *soju* may sometimes be served. Faced with a number of alcoholic drinks, the best thing is to follow the principals, using the wineglass if they do, for example. Thereafter, it is not uncommon for there to be regular toasting during the meal. Sometimes this will involve everybody, but sometimes it will just be individuals who toast each other. In all-male company, this can become quite a competition, and men may feel much pressure to drink large amounts of strong liquor. It is customary to turn the empty glass upside down, to show that the contents have been consumed. In mixed company, there is likely to be less pressure to drink; women need not feel compelled to drink toasts—they can simply touch the glass to their lips.

As in other parts of East Asia, it has also been customary to exchange glasses when drinking as a mark of friendship. In recent years the practice has become less common because of the realization that such exchanges could spread diseases.

## RETURNING HOSPITALITY

When you leave a restaurant or bar, you will not normally need to worry about the bill if a Korean colleague has invited you. You are the guest and taking care of the bill is your Korean host's responsibility. Koreans generally do not like the Western custom of "eating together and paying separately." The best way to repay hospitality is to invite your Korean friends to dinner after you have been entertained a couple of times. Take advice on both venue and costs—the latter can be very high.

If your Korean counterpart is visiting your country, that may well be a better opportunity to repay hospitality, perhaps even in your own home.

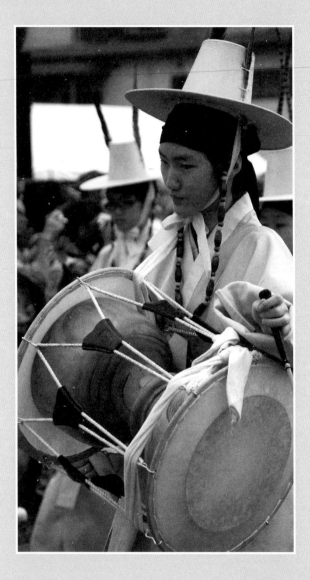

# CHAPTER SIX

# TIME OUT

Long working hours have become common in both Koreas. This is true even where there is not much work to do—to be at your place of work shows loyalty and dedication. There are differences of course. In the North, where the economic downturn of the 1990s destroyed much of the heavy industry and the jobs that went with it, people were still expected to turn up at their place of work but not to work late into the night. Office workers were perhaps expected to stay longer than factory workers. In the South, a cult of long hours meant that people did not leave offices until late in the evening. Until 1982, this, plus a midnight to 4.00 a.m. curfew, led many men not to go home at all. There have been changes but, in the South in particular, the cult of long hours is still prevalent.

This has an effect on how South Koreans entertain themselves. Many men, in particular, still go in for heavy drinking after work. Some people will spend most of the weekend catching up on sleep. Given the highly

Haeundae beach in Busan, South Korea.

developed electronics industry, video games played either at home or in special cafés are highly popular. But others go to theaters, to concerts or cinemas. At weekends, many take to the mountains that are everywhere on the peninsula. Picnics are a popular pastime in both North and South. Older people, men and women, seem to take a particular delight in such activities. Drink flows and they will often seek to draw passing foreigners into the dance. On the other hand, few people in the South "go away for the weekend"—the attitude is "Why would you? Everything you want is in the city." They might take a summer vacation in the mountains or, with millions of others, at the seaside. Skiing has become popular in winter.

In a change of trend, today, while many still spend their downtime at home, many young adults have taken to traveling, both within the country and overseas, whenever they can and however small the opportunity.

Social media has had a huge impact on the way young Koreans enjoy their leisure time. They find out about places to eat or travel to via television shows and Instagram, for example, and follow the latest trends and fashions, visiting hipster places such as cafés, restaurants, and shops made famous by the patronage of Korean celebrities or social media stars. It is mainly these celebrities who set the trend in lifestyles and fashion. Perhaps it is this vast sharing of information on social media that has given rise to the phenomenon of *hallyu*, or Korean wave (see page 117).

Holidays are rarer in the North, except for the highest levels of the elite. A short visit to a seaside or mountain resort every few years, organized by one's work unit, is a highly sought after privilege. City children may go with their school but families rarely go together.

Foreigners are not likely to participate in many of these activities, but if the chance arises it is worth taking for the insights it gives as well as the entertainment it provides. But there are plenty of ways for Koreans to find entertainment.

## ENTERTAINMENT IN THE SOUTH

Visitors or residents in South Korea will not lack for things to do. Activities range from eating and drinking in a bewildering range of establishments, through the opportunity to sample the highest international culture and a variety of museums and galleries, to floorshows

Playing the *chuk*, ritual percussion instrument.

of all types. Availability varies, of course. Seoul is very much at the apex in all that is on offer, and all interests are catered to in that city, but all the big cities will offer something.

Information about what is on is readily available. Seoul has had English-language newspapers for many years. The oldest are the *Korea Herald* and the *Korea Times*. The former was

Taepyeongmu, the traditional "Great Peace Dance."

long associated with the government, and the latter with the opposition, but it was hard to tell them apart. In recent years, not only have both gone online, but they have also been joined by other English-language papers, some linked to Korean dailies. They provide details of concerts and other forms of entertainment, which are also advertised on posters and billboards around the city.

In Seoul, the number of theaters and concert halls has increased steadily since the 1970s, stimulated by economic success and international events such as the 1988 Olympic Games. Even in the 1980s, it was said that there was a performance of Shakespeare in one or other of Seoul's many theaters every night of the year. By now, there must be two or three. Much experimental theater can also be found. Korea did not develop in theatrical terms as did Japan and China, and nothing quite

Pansori musical storyteller performance.

matches Kabuki or Peking opera in the Korean tradition. But traditional mask dances and other folk traditions are widely performed and increasingly popular, as are the various styles of Korean traditional music, from stately court performances to the exuberant drumming of the farmers' bands. These are often packaged for foreigners, with a traditional Korean dinner accompanying the music and dance.

Koreans have taken to Western music in a big way, and performances abound. Classical Western music is also available on the radio, and sales of compact discs are very high; whether the artists are Korean or foreign, compact discs are a good bargain and an enjoyable souvenir. As well as numerous high-quality

Song So-Hee singing "Arirang," the unofficial unified national anthem.

The National Dance Company of Korea performing the "Grand Drum Ensemble."

indigenous orchestras and performers, there is a steady stream of famous international visitors to add to the variety. Foreign classical orchestras find an enthusiastic audience in Korea; the international pop scene is also well represented, and jazz, partly spurred on by the large American presence in the country, has many outlets. Korean bands and pop music (K-pop) have a wide and dedicated following among the young and have acquired international status.

The appeal of K-pop and other cultural exports such as television shows, cinema, and Korean cuisine has become so influential that it has been given the Chinese name *hallyu*, or Korean wave, by the rest of the world. In North Korea, where officially all material from the

BtoB boy band on the music program M Countdown.

South is banned, there are reports that Korean wave material is widely available and watched clandestinely.

The cinema is very popular, and Seoul has many movie houses. Korea's film industry, which dates back to the 1920s, has begun to win international prizes—the metaphorical black comedy *Parasites* won the Palme d'Or in 2019 and Best Picture award at the 2020 Oscars—and many foreign films are also shown to enthusiastic local audiences. Once foreign films were dubbed into Korean, but today this is no longer the case, except on television. Today, foreign films shown to a Korean audience will have subtitles. Since the end of military dominance in politics, foreign films dealing with political themes are no longer banned.

Art galleries are also plentiful, covering traditional Korean styles of art and much more besides. A vibrant tradition of

The Sonamoo girl band opening the Korea Sale Festa.

experimental art, once frowned upon by the authorities, now attracts wide audiences. Foreign art is widely available today, in contrast even with the early 1990s.

Seoul has an abundance of museums. There are museums devoted to *kimchi*, the essential Korean condiment, to stones, to wrapping clothes, and to a host of other specialized interests. Most universities have museums, which, in the case of private establishments such as Korea or Yonsei universities, may reflect the particular interests of the founders. There is a fascinating National Folk Museum in the grounds of Seoul's Kyongbok Palace, which traces the life and customs of people of all classes and occupations up to the end of Korea's independence in 1910. Not to be missed is the Korean War Memorial, part shrine, part museum, which has been built on a former part of the United States military base at Yongsan. It takes as its theme all of Korea's past conflicts, not just the 1950–53 Korean War. Seoul's Museum of History in Jongno, which chronicles the history of the city, is well worth a visit. As well as permanent displays, it has a regular series of ad hoc exhibitions on special aspects of the capital. Another new museum, dealing with contemporary history, opened in 2012.

Outside Seoul, there are many museums to be found throughout the country, in addition to the local branches of the National Museum. Again, many are based in universities, but they can also be found in monasteries and at historic sites.

The main hall of Kyongbok Palace, Seoul.

## THE SOUTH KOREAN NATIONAL MUSEUM

The National Museum of Korea is a countrywide establishment, with the main museum in Seoul and branch museums in all the major cities. The best of these is probably that at Kyongju in the southeast, but all are worth a visit. Once they were quite old-fashioned in their presentations, but increasingly they are being rebuilt or updated, with modern styles of display and layout.

The Seoul museum has suffered because of political decisions. Originally established in 1908 in the final years of the Yi dynasty, it was developed by the Japanese. In 1945, the museum became the National Museum of Korea, with buildings in the Kyongbok Palace in Seoul. During the Korean War, the North Koreans intended to take all its holdings to the North in 1950, but Seoul's recapture took place before they could do so, and the museum, like the government, sat out the war in Pusan. At the end of the war, it moved back to Seoul, and in 1972 moved into a new building in the Kyongbok Palace grounds. However, in 1986, the Museum moved to the former Japanese administrative offices, known as the Capitol Building, in front of the Kyongbok Palace. This made a surprisingly good museum. For the first time, most of the collection was on display. In 1994, however,

President Kim Young Sam decided that the Capitol Building was too painful a symbol of the colonial past, and decreed that it should be destroyed. The museum, whose staff were not consulted, was forced to move into temporary buildings, its former building in the palace grounds having become the Folk Museum. A new building, situated on the former US forces Korea golf course at Yongsan, opened in October 2005, and has become very popular.

The collection is very rich, especially in archaeological materials from the various excavations of royal tombs throughout the peninsula. It is strong in statues of the Buddha, and in Korean painting.

Porcelain jar with red bamboo decoration.

For those staying longer in Seoul, the Korea Branch of the Royal Asiatic Society (KBRAS), originally founded in 1900, runs a regular series of lectures on the culture and history of the peninsula. The society's membership over the years has included most of the well-known names in Korean scholarship, including many prominent Korean scholars. It publishes an annual volume of Transactions, which is the oldest journal in the world devoted to Korean studies. In addition to its lecture series, which is aimed at the non-expert, KBRAS has regular excursions to scenic and historic sites throughout South Korea (and nowadays to China and other neighboring countries as well). These outings, with knowledgeable guides, are a good way to see the more unusual aspects of the country and also to get to know both Koreans and the resident foreign community.

Ink and water color painting by Jeong Seon.

## SPORTS

Both traditional and modern sports are available. The former includes Korean-style wrestling, *ssireum*, and *taekwondo*, the Korean version of unarmed combat. The latter is also a popular participation sport among foreigners. Spectator sports include baseball, and more recently, soccer, especially since the 2002 Football World Cup, jointly hosted by the Republic of Korea and Japan. The World Cup created much local enthusiasm (also echoed in North Korea), and soccer is now firmly established as a Korean sport. Several Korean players from both Koreas have become international stars. The armed forces play rugby, but this sport does not otherwise have much of a domestic following except among expatriates. Horse racing enjoys some popularity, as does horse riding.

*Ssireum* wrestling during a festival in Seoul.

Skiing, which became popular in the late 1970s and early 1980s, has taken off in a big way, with several world-class ski resorts, most within easy reach of Seoul. Once accommodation and other facilities were relatively simple, but today they reach the highest international standards. The season lasts from December to early March, although the resorts open from the end of November. The 2018 Winter Olympics were held in the ROK.

Golf is probably the most popular sport in South Korea, even if many of those who claim to be golfers rarely get beyond the driving ranges that can be found in the cities. Golf can be very expensive; it has always been especially popular among the industrial leaders of the country, perhaps in imitation of their Japanese counterparts. As in Japan, it can be particularly expensive for the outsider, and most foreign residents probably only play when invited by a Korean host. That said, if you have golf clubs and expect to do business, bring them to Korea. Many hotels have links to golf courses, and their guests can play on them. A lot of business can be done on the golf course, and Koreans are usually very pleased to find that a foreigner shares their passion for the game.

## FARTHER AFIELD

There is a huge range of scenic spots to visit, from Cheju Island in the south to the mountains of the east coast. All over South Korea, the discerning traveler will find places of amazing scenic beauty, with landscapes (and seascapes) that change dramatically with each season. Hiking trails snake up into the hills, or along coastal paths. Temples or hermitages—whose sites, if not the present buildings, often date back a thousand years or more—are to be found everywhere. Not only are the buildings attractive, with their curving roofs and stone pagodas, but since they provide popular destinations for Koreans, they will also give you a good opportunity to see Koreans enjoying themselves. And they do, singing, dancing, and drinking, men and women— and foreigners, if they can be dragged into the fun!

Areas once restricted, especially on the east coast, because of fear of North Korean infiltrators, are now readily available to Koreans and visitors alike. The east

The seaside temple of Haedong in Busan, South Korea.

coast has splendid beaches, with miles of golden sands. The west coast is equally attractive, with small islands—some tidal—situated close inshore. A steady increase in the number of National Parks has been accompanied by major improvements in access, facilities, and accommodation.

## SHOPPING

Shopping can be great fun in South Korea, whether in the big cities, with their smart department stores and numerous markets, or in small local markets. Leather and brass products are of a high standard. The range of goods available is huge, with electronic goods especially popular. Electronic goods can be purchased at very competitive prices at Yongsan Electronics Market in Seoul, a hub of more than 5,000 electronics stores spread across twenty buildings. Country markets may specialize in excellent traditional products, such as the bamboo goods at the village of Tamyang in South Cholla province. While prices may be fixed in the big department stores, they are not in the markets or in other shops, such as those in Itaewon near Seoul's main American base, and bargaining is quite normal. In Itaewon, shops and services such as tailors have grown accustomed to providing for the US military and their families and will stock or supply goods in larger sizes. Even though South Koreans are becoming bigger as they move from the traditional diet to a more Westernized one, they are still generally smaller than their Western counterparts.

Itaewon is also a center for traditional Korean-style furniture. Real antiques can be found in the area known as "Mary's Alley," near the Kyongbok Palace in the city center, but they are expensive. You are unlikely to find a real antique in Itaewon except at comparable prices to Mary's Alley, but a wide range of copies, some good, some less so, will be available.

You will find bookshops selling foreign-language books, including books about Korea, at a number of places in Seoul. The Kyobo Book Center is a vast underground shop right in the heart of the city. As well as books, it has CDs, computer software, and stationery. Another good bookshop is at the Ulchiro 1-ga subway station. Seoul Selection is both an on-line bookstore (http://www.seoulselection.com/) and a real shop in downtown Seoul. The Royal Asiatic Society Korea Branch publishes and sells books; they are available at a discount to members.

Duty-free shops, with international brands and high-quality Korean goods, are available in several big cities, as well as at the international airports. Prices are comparable to those elsewhere.

Some visitors may like to try two traditional Korean experiences—the barbershop and the bath. Korean barbershops can be very pleasant. You may not be able to appreciate the political and other gossip, but the combination of haircut, shave, and massage that usually features in a Korean barbershop's repertoire is quite an experience. It is a good idea, however, to stick to barbershops in hotels or other central locations.

Sometimes other establishments can be a front for prostitution. As such, they have been the target of frequent government campaigns against "lewd practices."

Korean public baths are similar to those found in Japan, with large communal bathtubs. Where they survive, they will now often offer specialized pools. As South Korea becomes wealthier, they are being supplanted by similar, but more expensive, "saunas," often in the bigger hotels. Public baths are segregated. They are friendly places, where inhibitions disappear. As in Japan, you must soap and rinse yourself thoroughly several times before entering the main bath. Again, as in Japan, this is likely to be at a hotter temperature than you are accustomed to, and you should be careful. Sit still and the pain eases! Many baths are equipped with saunas and resting rooms. In certain parts of the country, a variant of the bath is the hot spring, where natural water provides a means of relaxation and rejuvenation. Hot springs can be found all over the country, and today they are often fitness centers with elaborate gym facilities.

## THE NORTH

North Korea is rather more limited in what it has to offer, and visitors will have far less choice in what they do or see. That said, more cities and scenic spots are opening for foreign tourism. Much will depend on what you have asked to see before you go, though some sites tend to be a standard feature of all tours. All visitors will be accompanied by one or more guides. Their role is to make your visit as smooth as possible, but they will also try to ensure that you do not see or do anything that the authorities would rather you did not. Some guides ("minders" is the more pejorative term) can be helpful and understanding. Most will err on the side of caution with you. Remember, even if your guide is not around, other people will be watching you. It is also sensible to accept that the rules in the DPRK are different from those at home or in other countries. However petty or even silly they appear, it is best to stick to them.

Of course, there are museums and art galleries, especially in Pyongyang. It is not easy just to visit these. Indeed, the only museum that seems to accept the casual visitor without advance warning is the Folk Museum, near Kim Il Sung Square. This is smaller than its Seoul counterpart, but equally good in its depiction of life from prehistoric times to the end of the Yi dynasty in 1910. Other museums include the History Museum, the Revolutionary War Museum, and the Fatherland Liberation War Museum, devoted to the Korean War. The latter has doubled in size in recent years. As in most of the country's museums, visitors are taken on brief tours and see only a fraction of what is on display. All are worth a visit, although the displays may seem old-fashioned to most Westerners. There are also art galleries, and you can visit the display center of the Three Revolutions (in arts, science, and philosophy) by arrangement.

Pyongyang has many set-piece monuments, to which visitors are taken. Most prominent is the large gilded statue of Kim Il Sung, joined by Kim Jong Il since 2012, that stands on Mansu Hill. Here Koreans and foreigners come to lay flowers before the Leaders. One can decline to do so, but your North Korean hosts may be disappointed at such an action. They will, in any case, expect you to behave with decorum. Other sites associated with Kim Il Sung to which visitors are likely to be taken include the Arch of Triumph, marking the spot where he is supposed to have addressed the citizens of Pyongyang on liberation in 1945, his family home just outside the city at Mangyongdae, and the Kumsusan Palace of the Sun, where the embalmed bodies of Kim Il Sung and Kim Jong Il lie in state. Kumsusan, which was originally Kim Il Sung's office and home, is open twice a week, and foreigners are welcome. A visit involves

The Monument to National Reunification, south of Pyongyang.

elaborate checks and controls, to make sure that no contamination enters the building. Visitors should also be neatly dressed, with no bare arms. Be warned that overcoats, scarves, and hats must all be given up on entry. Visitors with pacemakers should be careful that they are exempted from the x-ray machines and wands that are in use. The officials understand and will do a body check if required. Visiting Mangyongdae is more relaxed. It is set in an attractive park, with pleasant walks. At these and other monuments and historic sites a guide will provide the official account of what is deemed significant.

Despite journalists' descriptions of it as a "Stalinist city," Pyongyang has much to recommend it. There are many parks and green spaces, and delightful riverside walks along the Taedong and the Potong Rivers. On weekends, people will be picnicking, with dancing and singing, just as they would be in the South. Overzealous minders sometimes prevent visitors from just wandering

Panorama of central Pyongyang.

about. Shopping is not the delight that it is in South Korea. Foreigners may visit shops out of curiosity, but most find that there is little they would want to buy, even if they could. Posters, available at the Foreign Languages Bookshop and some other outlets, make attractive gifts. However, those same overzealous guides have been known to deny the existence of the bookshop, and the realization that such products can get a good price internationally has led to restrictions on sales. Persistence may be required to visit it. There is a duty-free shop at Pyongyang airport, with a selection of liquors, and also a general souvenir shop and a bookshop.

The theater, a musical performance, or one of the two circuses make good outings, but may not always be available, especially in winter, when such places of entertainment are not heated. It is always worth asking, however. The "revolutionary operas," which perhaps owe more to the Chinese tradition and to Hollywood

Scene from the revolutionary opera *Red Detatchment of Women*.

than to any Korean one, are well staged and very dramatic. If foreigners are attending, the texts may be projected in English at the side of the stage.

Occasionally, you will come across a poster for a concert or some similar event, but finding out what is on, and what may be available for foreigners, is no easy task. "Keep asking" seems to be the rule.

What are called "mass games" or "mass gymnastic performances" are worth seeing. Thousands of people working together provide spectacular set pieces based on the exploits of Kim Il Sung or other aspects of recent history. After a gap of some years, the Mass Games were revived in 2018 to mark the seventieth anniversary of the establishment of the DPRK, under the title of "The Glorious Country." This provided a somewhat stylized account of Korean history as seen from a North Korean perspective. As well as the use of flash cards and large numbers of performers, it used computer-generated graphics and other up-to-date techniques. Otherwise, nightlife is generally confined to restaurants and hotel bars, selling a variety of local and imported beers and spirits. There are restaurants and bars on some boats moored along the Taedong River, which provide an attractive setting on a summer's evening.

Away from Pyongyang, the scenery is every bit as stunning as that in the South, though there is nothing like the South's tourist infrastructure. The Kumgang or Diamond Mountains on the east coast, one of Korea's most famous beauty spots, which were not accessible to foreigners while the Hyundai Company's tours operated up to 2008, are now again open. Not much in the way of historic buildings survived the Korean War, but there are some reconstructed temples and hermitages. Mount Myohyang, about 75 miles (120 km) north of Pyongyang, has some Buddhist remains, excellent hill walking, and two museums devoted to preserving the gifts given to Kim Il Sung and Kim Jong Il. All are worth visiting. Kaesong, on the division between North and South, not only provides access to the truce village of Panmunjom but is also one of the few North Korean towns to have preserved many of its older buildings. Kaesong was the capital during the Koryo period (918–1392) and there are royal tombs and other remains in the area. Not the least of its delights is a hotel set in traditional buildings. Kaesong's museum is also set in an ancient building. Near to Kaesong are temples and hiking trails well worth exploring.

# CHAPTER SEVEN

# TRAVEL, HEALTH, & SAFETY

Traveling is very different in the two Koreas. The South is well provided with modern transportation facilities, including high-speed trains, intercity buses, and a network of domestic air routes. Many cities have metro railways. English is widely used in the transportation system, which makes individual travel easy. Facilities can be crowded, and Koreans are not averse to pushing and shoving, although foreigners will often find that they are deferred to and certainly helped if apparently lost.

The North's travel infrastructure is improving but it has along way to go. Rail links are patchy at best. There are no long-distance buses and a rudimentary domestic air network. Individual travel by foreigners is not possible except on the international train to Beijing. One is always accompanied by a guide or guides who will make the arrangements and accompany the party, whether it is one or twenty.

## GETTING AROUND IN THE SOUTH

Visiting South Korea is relatively straightforward.
Most Western countries have visa waiver arrangements
with the Republic of Korea, usually allowing visits
of up to ninety days. Those going for work will
need visas, but these are easily obtained from ROK
Embassies around the world. As noted, Cheju has its
own visa arrangements.

South Korea has a modern and highly developed
transportation system. Most visitors will arrive at the
Inch'on International Airport, a stunningly designed
facility opened in 2000 that won the Best International
Airport award every year from 2005 to 2015 and
continues to receive international accolades. Its only
drawback is that it is not yet on the subway system.
A high-speed train called AREX (Airport Railroad
Express) links the airport to Seoul railway station
(between 43 and 53 minutes). Taxis and buses provide
frequent links to Inch'on city, where the subway system
runs, or to the center of Seoul. There are also regional
international flights to and from Pusan and some
other airports. Seoul's former international airport,
Kimpo, became a domestic hub after 2001, but has
recently begun to be used for some international
flights. It is close to the city center and has subway
connections. South Korea's main carriers are Korean
Air, the oldest, and Asiana Airlines, but many major
airlines also serve the country, with a small number
flying to Pusan as well. EastStar is a budget airline. Air

Inch'on Internatioal Airport railway station.

Busan serves the southeast region. Departure tax is included in the price of the ticket.

## Boats

A few people come by ship to Inch'on. Some passengers travel to North Korea by taking a ferry to Dandong on the Chinese side of the Yalu River, and then crossing to the North Korean city of Shinuiju to catch the train. From Pusan, there are ferries to Japan. Ferries also connect the Korean mainland with Ullung Island in the East Sea and with Cheju and other islands off the south coast. They can be a fun way to travel and get to know people. They may not have much in the way of comfort, however, and the seas both east and south can often be rough.

## Trains

Railways began to appear at the start of the twentieth century and were much expanded during the Japanese period. They suffered badly during the Korean War, and the modern railway system is smaller than its prewar predecessor. That said, most main cities are accessible by rail. Seoul and Pusan are linked, since April 2004, by a fast French-designed bullet train, which has reduced the journey time to two hours and forty minutes from the previous four hours. Not only are these trains modern and fast, they are also cheap by European or North American standards. A single first-class fare to Pusan is about £25–40, or US $40–60, depending on the type of train. Visitors can purchase

Korean Rail passes outside the country, allowing unlimited travel for set periods, which further reduces the cost.

## Road Transportation

The modern road system also dates from the Japanese period. Korean roads were traditionally very bad. In the 1950s and 1960s, it was easier to fly to many places than to drive, and many small airports sprang up all over the country. Even in the 1980s, a surprisingly high proportion of roads were still dirt tracks, but this began to change in the lead-in to the 1988 Seoul Olympics. A major construction program that started in the early 1970s saw the spread of modern high-speed roads. This also led to a countrywide system of fast buses, which provided a much cheaper service than by air, and many airports were closed.

But from the mid-1980s onward, the pendulum swung again in favor of flying. Car purchase, hitherto very expensive, was encouraged to boost the faltering automobile manufacturers, and car ownership became widespread. As a result, the sheer volume of traffic on the roads has often reduced progress to a miserable crawl. This was especially the case at major festivals, such as the fall harvest festival, Chusok, or Lunar New Year, when many people return to their ancestral homes. Friday and Sunday evenings are still likely to produce major jams, especially around Seoul, so the wise traveler will avoid the roads.

Within cities too, the volume of traffic means that journeys by road can be very slow and time-consuming. It is possible to rent cars, with an international driver's license, but visitors contemplating doing so should remember that the Korean style of driving is somewhat different from that practiced elsewhere, and parking may be a difficulty. Many middle-class Koreans still have chauffeurs, so parking is less of a worry for them, but somebody unfamiliar with Seoul or Pusan may well find themselves experiencing problems. Traffic police were once indulgent toward foreigners who parked illegally or badly, but those days have gone. If you do decide to drive, finding your way about is not such a problem, as most signs include names in roman script. Be warned that U-turns are only allowed at certain designated points, and you may sometimes have to go well out of your way to make one.

All major South Korean cities have good bus services, though they, too, suffer from the density of traffic. Many foreigners use the buses, though it is useful to have some knowledge of Korean to do so, since destination boards are not usually in roman letters. Be warned that bus stops are often a long way apart—miss your stop and you will have a long walk back!

## The Subway

By far the best way to travel is the subway system, especially in Seoul, where the subways provide

comprehensive coverage of the city. Inch'on, Pusan,
Taegu, Kwangju, and Taejon also have subway systems,
but none is as highly developed as that of Seoul. This
began in 1974 and now has 22 lines and 707 stations.
The total length is 179.4 miles (287 km). The lines
stretch well out into the suburbs, and even to outlying
cities such as Uijongbu and Inch'on. The stations are
well designed, with maps and information in English.
They are often also linked to the underground
shopping arcades that are such a feature of Korean
cities. As in other cities, the subways can become very
crowded at the morning and evening rush hours; the
wise traveler avoids such times. They can also be very
full in the late evenings, as the businessmen (and a
few women) make their way home. This is a time to
be careful. Just occasionally, a drunken passenger may
take exception to a foreigner, especially if the latter is a
man with a Korean woman, or a woman who appears
to be Korean. Anti-American outbursts are not
unknown on the subways in the evenings. It is best not
to talk too loudly or to draw attention to oneself.

## Taxis

South Korean cities are well supplied with taxis. In
Seoul, these come in a variety of styles and prices;
the bigger and cleaner the car, the more expensive
it will be, and the more likely it will be to have a
driver who understands some English and who
will charge the correct fare. It is a good idea to have
destinations written out by a Korean, since foreigners'

pronunciation is often difficult for Koreans to understand. Cab-call services are available through smartphone applications such as Kakaotalk, which has an inbuilt function called Kakaotaxi for calling a taxi.

### Walking

While there are parts of all South Korean cities that are pleasant to explore on foot, such as market areas, and in Seoul the historic center, most cities are not particularly good for walking. There are few historic buildings and the general quality of architecture is not high, although there are some exceptions. Amenities such as public toilets used to be rare, but, especially in Seoul, availability has much improved as a result of a series of international events beginning with the 1986 Asian Games. These events have also led to improvements in facilities to help the disabled.

Those on foot need to be careful late at night in certain areas. Physical violence against foreigners is still rare, but, as with the subway system, late night drunks, however apparently respectable, can be abusive. Whatever the temptation, it is probably best for a foreigner to keep out of Korean quarrels.

Walking and hiking are possible, especially in the mountains. These are everywhere; even Seoul has mountains within the city boundaries. Intensive agriculture can hinder the walker in the countryside, and one must be very careful not to damage the dykes around the paddy fields. Seoul has its cross-country running clubs, including the Hash House Harriers, who welcome newcomers.

## GETTING AROUND IN THE NORTH

Most travelers to North Korea arrive at Pyongyang's International Airport, Sunan, just outside the city. The only regular carrier is the national airline, Air Koryo, which flies to Beijing twice a week, and also serves Shenyang in northeast China and the Russian Far East. Chinese airlines also fly at busier periods. The other main route is by rail from China. The journey takes about twenty hours to or from Beijing, but travelers should be aware that the train can often be delayed, especially in the summer rainy season. The third permitted route is across the Tumen River to the special economic zone at Rason (formerly Rajin-Sonbong), in the far northeast of the country. It is not easy to get to Pyongyang from there. Routes to Russia are being opened but it is not yet clear whether they will be open to tourists.

All visitors to North Korea need to be hosted by a local organization, either Korean or a foreign organization such as an embassy or UN agency. For tourists, this will be the (North) Korean National Tourist Organization. Visitors also need a visa. This, except in very rare circumstances, must be obtained outside the country. Most people use the DPRK Embassy in Beijing (near Ritan Park in the east of the city), but if there is a DPRK Embassy in your country, you can get a visa there. It is wise to allow at least a month and probably longer to obtain your visa. In the past tourist visas were difficult to obtain for citizens of some countries, including the United States. Since 2010, however, most prohibitions appear to have been lifted, except for South Korean and Israeli citizens. Since 2017, the US government has banned its citizens from traveling to the DPRK, but this may change. It is important to check in advance. The cost of visas varies. The North Koreans argue that they charge visitors on a scale relating to what North Koreans are charged. If your country charges US $30, a North Korean visa will cost you US $30. In practice, the rates charged seem to vary somewhat. While visas are not required for the Rajin-Sonbong Economic Zone in the northeast of the country, visitors are required to obtain a letter authorizing their visit. The procedures for this are just as cumbersome as for a visa.

It is best also to avoid bringing in publications in Korean and those relating to North Korea. The North Koreans are generally not happy with much that is written about their country and may confiscate material relating to the peninsula. This includes guidebooks. Religious publications are also viewed with suspicion; they are best left behind. You will be expected to fill out a customs form listing valuables, publications, cameras, cell phones, and currency. Be warned that they may check. Departure procedures may include a check on photographs or videos taken.

If the officials do not like what they see, you will have to delete it.

All visitors are met. Casual traveling is unheard of. Most visitors will have a Korean host waiting for them. Those joining or visiting embassies and international organizations will be met by representatives from those bodies. Do not panic if there appears to be nobody to greet you at first. They will arrive, but sometimes have trouble fighting their way through the waiting crowds. Nobody has ever been left completely unattended. The airport can be a bit daunting as people struggle to get themselves and their luggage through the checkpoints, although since the modernization program, completed in 2017, procedures have notably improved. It is best to relax and let things take their course. Luggage is rarely lost or left behind, but the airport staff may stack it up in a system known only to them. So, if something appears to have gone missing, ask your hosts to search thoroughly before panicking.

Once within North Korea, foreigners with Korean hosts are likely to find that they are kept on a tight rein. Those responsible for you take their duties very seriously and will often refuse to let you out of their sight. International driver's licenses are not accepted and there are no facilities for self-drive cars. Only resident foreigners who have taken a local driving test can drive; heads of international organizations and diplomatic missions are exempt from taking the test as long as they can produce a valid driver's license.

There are rental cars outside hotels and some shops. However, unless a Korean accompanies you, these may well refuse to take you. Note that they do not operate on Sundays.

All travel will be arranged. Because the railways are in a poor state as a result of lack of maintenance and general economic decline, journey times are long and unpredictable. The condition of the rolling stock is also poor. Most journeys, therefore, are done by road. Until recently, the cars provided were likely to be 1960s or 1970s vintage Volvos or Mercedes-Benz. More modern ones are increasingly available. All vehicles are poorly maintained—tires, in particular, are often very worn down—but the drivers do their best.

One hazard is that many drivers seem to drink. Refuse to go with a driver who has been drinking. In theory, it is illegal to drink and drive in North Korea, but many North Korean drivers seem blissfully unaware of this. Gradually, however, the traffic police seem to be becoming more diligent in watching out for such drivers. In another aid to safety, it is now compulsory for the driver and anybody in the front seat of a vehicle to wear a seat belt. More modern minibuses, often used for small tour groups, also seem to have seatbelts for passengers.

There are no intercity buses. Within most major cities there are buses, but foreigners are generally not taken on (or perhaps even allowed on) them. The same is true of the trams/light railways found in some cities, and of Pyongyang's extensive fleet of trams,

Jongwang metro station in Pyongyang.

buses, and trolleybuses. Foreigners do occasionally break the taboo, however. Pyongyang has a two-line subway system. Foreigners usually visit this as a tourist attraction rather than a means of transportation, though in theory it is open for use.

Walking around is often discouraged. Until recently, even resident foreigners outside Pyongyang (and in the early days of international aid, even within Pyongyang) were confined to hotels. Today resident foreigners and their guests usually have no problem. Resident foreigners may also use bicycles, but there are none available to rent.

Foreigners do go jogging in Pyongyang. Away from the cities, there is good hiking in the many mountain areas, but visitors are likely to be closely monitored and are unlikely to be allowed to go off on their own. Resident foreigners are in theory somewhat freer, but even they find that there are limits on where they can go.

## WINTER DRIVING

Finally, a note of caution on winter driving that applies to both North and South Korea. Winter driving can be dangerous. Snow and ice turn many roads into ice rinks. In some parts of South Korea, snow tires and chains may be required. The watchword must be care, but not all Korean drivers seem to be aware of the dangers, and sometimes drive too fast on icy roads.

In North Korea, it is the poor condition of the vehicles, combined with untreated roads, which poses the biggest danger. Do not hesitate to ask for drivers to go more slowly.

## WHERE TO STAY IN THE SOUTH

### Hotels
You will find that South Korea is very well served for hotel accommodation. The official ratings system lists hotels as super deluxe (SDL), deluxe (DL), first, second,

and third class, but these categories, according to the (South) Korean National Tourist Organization (KNTO), do not necessarily correspond to the classifications used in Western countries.

In Seoul and the other major cities there are many world-class hotels; they also come with world-class prices, and some are members of international chains. They have all the facilities and the standard of service you would expect from such a type of hotel; swimming pools, jogging paths, and high-class restaurants. The restaurants will include at least one Western restaurant, usually with a French-sounding name, Chinese and Japanese restaurants, and of course, a Korean restaurant. The rooms will be well appointed, with international television, access points for computers, and minibars. The latter can be very expensive. Robes and slippers are

Jungmun Saekdal Beach Hotel on Cheju Island.

invariably provided. Once, razors, toothbrushes, and other toiletries might also have been available, but this is less likely nowadays since the government has decreed that these are an unnecessary luxury. If you find yourself without a toothbrush, however, most hotels will happily provide one. Many hotels can be booked from abroad, via travel agents or through the Internet.

All such hotels will have a coffee shop, which serves simple meals and is often open both earlier and later than the standard restaurants, and any number of bars. "Irish" bars are enjoying a vogue in Seoul, just as in other parts of the world. Several of these hotels have special club floors as well, which, in addition to providing such business services as fax, Internet, and similar resources, will often have a private bar with a free "happy hour" period for drinks.

In the big cities such hotels are good places to eat, to meet people—most Koreans are very happy to meet and be seen in the major hotels—and even to do some modest shopping. If you cannot manage without a particular Western brand of toothpaste, for example, there is a chance that you will find it in such a place. Most have small bookshops and other more general outlets. Sometimes, the bookshops will turn up long-out-of-print works hard to find anywhere else. In Seoul, many of the central high-class hotels link up with the extensive network of underground shopping centers. These central hotels are also good venues from which to watch Koreans. They are often the choice for introducing young couples to each other, for example.

## "Tourist Hotels"

If you wish to be more adventurous, you should try some of the smaller and cheaper hotels. These are often described as "tourist hotels." They will have more simple facilities, but will usually have a Korean and a Chinese restaurant, and perhaps a coffee shop. The bars are likely to be brighter and brasher than the dark lounges of the more expensive places. Especially away from Seoul, they will often offer good value for money, and in some places they will be all that is available. The staff will be less sophisticated than in the international-class hotels but will usually be helpful and certainly friendly. Although simpler, there is no reason why small hotels should be any less comfortable than their more expensive counterparts.

## *"Yogwan"*

Even more modest are *yogwan*, or Korean inns. The Chinese characters read the same as the Japanese *ryokan* and mean simply "building for travelers." In practice, few Korean *yogwan* equate to the *ryokan*, either in style of building or standard of comfort. Only in the remoter islands or in some mountain areas is the visitor likely to come across a *yogwan* that is anything more than a concrete shell—but they can still be fun to stay in. Remember that in most *yogwan* the price includes at least dinner and breakfast—though do not be surprised if these two meals are more or less the same!

Sleeping arrangements vary in the *yogwan*. In some you will find a few rooms with Western-style beds; in others, you will sleep on the floor, Korean-style. In the latter case, there will be a mattress and a thick quilt, plus sheets. Whether you sleep on the floor or in a bed, you may find the traditional Korean pillows literally rather hard to take. Once they would have been wood or porcelain, but even today, they are hard. There is usually no rule about how many people stay in a Korean-style room. Just make it clear on checking in. Also remember that, as in a Korean house, shoes are not worn indoors.

Another thing to check is the standard of cleanliness. You will have no problems in top-class establishments, which are invariably spotless, but the same standards may not apply in more remote areas. Do not hesitate to ask for a room to be cleaned, or for clean sheets and pillowcases, if you suspect that those offered you have been used before.

## Youth Hostels

For travelers with very limited budgets, South Korea has some fifty-five youth hostels, all of which belong to the Korea Youth Hostel Association (KYHA). These hostels will be found in the major cities as well as in scenic areas. Visitors who are used to the relatively small-scale hostels of Europe are likely to be in for a surprise. The smallest has more than a hundred beds, while there are several very large ones with a thousand beds or more. Membership is required, though membership of a foreign YHA may be accepted. In order to guarantee a place, bookings should be made in advance.

## Home Stays

Home visits are a possibility in South Korea, although, except in the countryside, you are increasingly unlikely to stay in traditional Korean housing; it is much more probable that you will find yourself in one of the much-sought-after modern apartment blocks. The apartments have modern facilities, including toilets, baths, and central heating, and are much more secure than low-rise houses. As has been mentioned, some of the rules of traditional houses still apply within the modern apartment—you do not wear shoes, of course. Slippers will be provided for use in corridors and vestibules. You change these for a different set of slippers when using the toilet. Although the old division into men's and women's quarters is not possible in a modern apartment, it is sometimes quite rare to see the wife in such a home. She will be busy in the kitchen, even if there are staff to help prepare food, and may not even eat with the guests on whose behalf she has labored. For the foreign visitor, a home stay will provide a good introduction to Korean life.

If you get the opportunity to stay in a traditional house, take it! As is often the case in all types of Korean homes, life will be lived at floor level. In winter, the house will be heated by the under-floor system known as *ondol*. The hot gases from the kitchen fire are drawn under the floor to a chimney at the other side of the house. Floors can sometimes become very warm, which is fine on a snowy winter's morning, but can be a bit overpowering as winter gives way to spring. If you are

Bulguksa Temple on the slopes of Mount Toham.

staying in a remote area in a traditional house or inn with *ondol*, make sure that a window is open or that there is some other means of ventilation. Each year, carbon monoxide poisoning kills a few people because they have slept in tightly sealed rooms into which the gas has come though an undetected crack in the floor.

## Temples

For those who prefer something even more unusual, it may be possible to stay in a Buddhist temple. Because Buddhism was forced out of the cities during the long Yi dynasty (1392–1910), temples that survived tended to be in more remote, mountainous areas. Today, these are often prime tourist destinations, and so in recent years some temples have been taking in visitors for short stays, to experience, however briefly, the life of contemplation and ceremony practiced by the monks. There are also some temples that have traditionally accepted foreigners for greater or lesser periods. Such attachments involve following the full ascetic training of the monks.

## Longer Term

Longer-stay visitors, or even those taking up residence, might like to consider using a residence hotel, of which there are several in Seoul. Essentially these are fully furnished service apartments, sometimes attached to hotels. They will provide health club facilities, restaurants, and other requirements, such as Internet access, and also amenities, such as a kitchen, to allow one to lead a more independent life.

## WHERE TO STAY IN THE NORTH

Accommodation in North Korea offers much less choice. Pyongyang has a selection of hotels where foreign visitors are lodged, but in most other places that foreigners are able to visit there is one hotel that takes foreigners, and that is that. An exception is Kaesong, the former capital of the Koryo kingdom (918–1392). Kaesong has a considerable amount of charm, mainly because of the large number of traditional houses that survive. Today there are two hotels. One is a modern block, best avoided. The other is delightful, being made up of a series of old houses with small courtyards, traditional rooms, and modern facilities. If the opportunity arises, this is a good place to stay, and it has some of the best food in North Korea.

Pyongyang's hotels range from the supposedly deluxe Koryo and Yanggakdo Hotels to some very simple places, including one that is called a youth hostel. The prices are relatively high and the quality of service has been low, but there are signs of improvement. A major change in Pyongyang's hotels is the increasing availability of international satellite television, but there are other positive developments as well. At one time, the Koryo Hotel rooms could not be locked, for example, but this has now changed. Cleanliness can also be a problem, as can supplies of hot water in hotels away from Pyongyang. Hot water may be limited to short periods in the morning and evening, and you may have to indicate which you prefer.

Various government ministries also have guesthouses for senior foreign visitors. These are likely to be more attractive places to stay than the hotels, since they are often set in gardens or other pleasant surroundings, but they suffer from two main disadvantages: they are sometimes remote from the city center, and they are guarded—so much so that visitors may find that they cannot leave the grounds. Also, while bedrooms will be kept warm in winter, public areas, including restaurants, are often not heated at all. This can be something of a shock in January and February.

## HEALTH

### The South

Standards of health care are high in South Korea. There are excellent, if expensive, hospitals, available in all major cities. Many physicians and dental surgeons have trained abroad, often in the United States. Western-style medicinal drugs are readily available and in regular use. Some foreigners have found that South Korean doctors tend to overprescribe. Make sure you have adequate supplies of any medical needs, as well as insurance.

Water is generally safe, and bottled water is widely available for those who prefer it. Cholera, once common, is now rare, as are malaria and encephalitis. However, since malaria has reappeared in North Korea, it is wise to take precautions against mosquito bites. Avoid uncooked food, and be cautious about hotel buffets, where food may sit around for a long time.

## The North

The visitor to North Korea should be aware that health care can be somewhat precarious. Many North Korean physicians have been well trained either in North Korea, Eastern Europe, or the former Soviet Union. But lack of funds and ideological differences mean that most of that training would have taken place a long time ago, so North Korean doctors today are unfamiliar with current medical practices. Conditions such as malaria, once eradicated, have come back in recent years. This will not affect visitors to the main cities, but anyone going into the countryside should be aware of the problem.

In addition, the economic decline of recent years has hit the health service badly. Few hospitals, even in Pyongyang, have up-to-date equipment, and most lack facilities such as X-ray machines, general anesthetics, and drugs. North Koreans are helpful when there is a problem, but in general, any medical or dental emergency will involve a speedy departure from the

DPRK. Make sure that vaccinations are up-to-date and that you have immunization for Hepatitis A and B and typhoid. Bring a first aid kit, which should include simple preparations for stomach upsets and common medicines such as aspirin. The latter may sometimes be available, but there is no guarantee. Bring an adequate supply of prescription drugs. It makes sense to bring supplies of contraceptives and sanitary needs. Sanitary towels may be available but it is unlikely that tampons will be found. In case of serious injury or accident, medical evacuation may be necessary, so comprehensive travel insurance is essential.

Tap water is not safe. Bottled water is widely available. Avoid uncooked food.

### COVID-19
Given the proximity of China, where COVID-19 first emerged in December 2019, it was not surprising that the pandemic quickly spread to the Korean Peninsula. In South Korea, the first case was reported on 20 January. In late February a massive program of testing and quarantine began, with restrictions on travelers from affected countries, and an effective tracing program was introduced. By early May the disease was thought to be sufficiently contained to allow the lifting of controls. However, there were soon major spikes of infection linked to nightclubs and places of worship. The government's response was swift and, despite the setbacks, its handling of the crisis was widely viewed as exemplary. It also led to a surge in support for President Moon.

North Korea's initial claims that it had no cases of COVID-19 were viewed with scepticism by many outsiders. As with past epidemics, the country adopted drastic preventative measures in January, including widespread quarantine, with the closure of schools and colleges, and an almost total ban on travel, including to and from China. In both countries tourism came to a complete halt.

## SAFETY

Most foreigners visiting or living in either North or South Korea have found that they are perfectly safe. Crime rates are low and foreigners are rarely targeted. A few possible dangers have been noted in passing such as the occasional drunk who takes exception to a foreign man and an apparently Korean woman. In Pyongyang, my successor, the first British ambassador, had his golf clubs stolen from his car parked outside the Koryo Hotel. Generally however, the tales are of dropped wallets or discarded items being returned. Even the ambassador got his clubs back!

Winter driving can be dangerous, and it is wise to wear seatbelts in both cars and buses. The police are generally helpful, but it may be hard to find an officer who speaks a foreign language. One area to be careful of is the Sino–North Korean border area. On the Chinese side there are groups and organizations operating that are best avoided. They include a variety of intelligence and security agencies, smugglers both of people and goods, all of which should be given a wide berth.

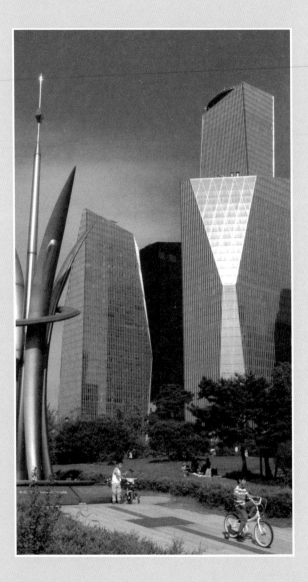

# CHAPTER EIGHT

# BUSINESS BRIEFING

The rapid transformation of South Korea has taken the country from poverty in the 1950s to the world's eleventh largest economy by the 1990s. After the setback of the 1997 Asian economic crisis, South Korea bounced back. Reforms introduced then enabled the country to ride out the global financial crisis of 2008 and to emerge in good shape. In 2009, it was the first former recipient of international development assistance to become a significant aid donor. In 2012, it ranked fifteenth in nominal GDP terms, or twelfth in purchasing parity. There are challenges ahead, with an ageing workforce, a heavy dependence on exports, and increasing competition from China, but few doubt that it will succeed in meeting these challenges.

Rapid economic development has meant that more and more foreigners do business with the country. In many ways, this proves no more difficult than doing business anywhere else. Your Korean counterparts are likely to be as well-educated and experienced as you are—many South Koreans have studied in Europe and North America, and some will have lived abroad. The first generation of Korea's business leaders, the heads of the *chaebol*, or industrial conglomerates, may not have had much exposure to the outside world in their youth, but their successors are sophisticated and experienced. This is less the case in the North, but even there more exposure to the outside world is beginning to change attitudes and style. Nevertheless, the Koreans do some things slightly differently from businesses in the West. If you have negotiated in China or Japan, you will soon recognize a kinship with the Koreans.

## CONFUCIAN VALUES

Some describe these common characteristics as "Confucian," but, as one academic writer has noted, the trouble with "Confucianism" is that it is as full of contradictions as any other set of beliefs that have developed over long periods of time and in very different environments. A complicating factor is that the Confucian canon put the merchant in a low position in the hierarchy, which does not square with the respect paid to successful businessmen in Korea today. While the behavior of some South Korean modern industrialists may correspond to Confucian precepts, that of others does not.

That said, you will hear the term used to describe Korean business practices. This tends to mean that

Koreans value hierarchy, with age receiving more respect than youth, prefer order to chaos, have a high regard for education, dislike ostentation, and emphasize the group rather than the individual. It also includes a belief in the value of hard work.

## WOMEN IN BUSINESS

Another aspect of Confucianism that has undoubtedly affected Korea is the attitude toward women. Women ranked low in the Confucian hierarchy. Such attitudes have taken a long time to change. Korean women fight against such discrimination and are increasingly making their presence felt in areas traditionally dominated by men. But they still have some way to go and do not yet occupy many senior positions in business or industry. Non-Korean women benefit from being outsiders to whom the normal rules do not apply, but they may well feel that they are not being treated as the equals of their male counterparts.

Kim Sung Joo, founder of the Sungjoo Group.

## FACE

Then there is "face." This is almost as hard to define as Confucianism itself. In some ways, it boils down to avoiding doing or saying something that will embarrass your Korean counterpart in front of others. Remember that it is not only the person who is embarrassed who loses "face." The person perpetuating the deed has also done so because they have put somebody else in an impossible position. The way to handle difficult situations is to avoid direct confrontation or blame in front of others, and then to tackle the issue in private. So, do not tell a person that he or she is lying, even if you know that to be the case. Take them aside and explain that your understanding of the position is different from theirs. This allows both of you to move around the problem, and, with luck, to find a solution.

This same principle applies to business negotiations. Try always to avoid being negative, and never rule anything out. A soft answer can often produce a solution; the other side does not want you to lose face either.

It follows that anger, or the appearance of anger, should be avoided as far as possible. The Confucian gentleman does not get angry—although he may get even.

Business gifts are also a matter of face. As in Japan, the giving and receiving of presents is a very important part of social behavior. Gifts are expected as a means of showing sincerity. Give the right present, and you have shown that you understand the position of the recipient. This is not so much a matter of expense as of quality and appropriateness. If you are not sure, consult a Korean.

## FORMALITY

The Korean approach to business is more formal than is now customary in the West. Those engaged in business should dress and act the part; informality is not a Korean characteristic. Set-piece negotiations are common, with large groups on either side of the table. Normally, however, only the principals on each side will speak. The others are there for consultations if necessary, and perhaps to give advice in writing as the meeting progresses. Koreans will not be impressed if junior members of a team intervene unbidden.

Formality may sometimes spill over into social occasions associated with business. At a cocktail party, do not expect older people to talk to younger ones, and do not be surprised if it is hard to get much out of junior members on the Korean side. Sometimes the alcohol invariably consumed on such occasions will break down the barriers, but not always, especially if the Korean host is particularly senior. If you are invited to a bar, however, then the atmosphere will be more relaxed, and the consumption of alcohol even higher.

## BUSINESS DRESS SENSE

Koreans tend to dress formally during the working week. This applies to North and South, and to both men and women. Men will generally wear somber-colored Western suits. There are some exceptions, especially in South Korea. Among academics, for instance, it is not unusual to find sports jackets, though usually of a fairly conservative style and color. An artist may wear a French-style beret and have a beard. In some of the bigger Korean companies, all staff, whether managerial or shop-floor workers, will wear the company uniform. During the hottest period in summer, some of this formality may be relaxed, and, for example, open-necked shirts will become the norm in government offices. If in doubt, however, a man should wear a tie.

Women will find that their Korean counterparts will dress conservatively. Bare shoulders are not acceptable, and short skirts are strictly for the young. Trousers and trouser suits are very popular among South Korean women, and a well-tailored pair of trousers will prove suitable dress for most occasions. This style is equally appropriate in North Korea, though, especially in Pyongyang, women normally wear skirts from about mid-March to mid-November.

Foreigners do not have to conform exactly to Korean standards, but for those doing business it is wise not to get out of line with Korean practice. Loud sports shirts and shorts are not acceptable for the office, or for formal calls, even in the hottest and stickiest weather.

Wearing clothes appropriate for the occasion is a mark of discernment. Koreans take leisure as seriously as work. If you are invited to play golf or tennis, it is important that you dress correctly. Even picnics and mountain climbing demand the right outfit. No matter that numerous Koreans wearing quite the wrong shoes and clothes for going up mountains will pass you; the real gentleman (and lady) will have good stout shoes, a proper hat, and a stout stick. Again, Koreans will appreciate it if you have made the effort. In any case, such equipment makes sense on the surprisingly rugged hills of Korea. Low they may be, but easy they are not!

## INTRODUCTIONS

When introduced, you should bend your upper body slightly. Koreans generally bow sparingly, unlike the Japanese. Among men, you should also offer your hand. There are no hard and fast rules about who should offer a hand first. If two Koreans meet, the senior will generally make the first move, but the same rules do not apply to foreigners. It is less common for Korean women to shake hands.

## THE BUSINESS CARD

After the introduction, you should present your business card. Business cards are extensively used in both North and South Korea, and it is a good idea to have some even if you are only staying for a short while. You can of course have them printed at home, but there are advantages in waiting until you arrive in Korea. They can be prepared quickly, and Korean printers will add your name and address, or that of your company or organization, in Korean.

Cards should be offered with both hands if possible, or, if that is not possible, with the right hand. When receiving a card, it is good form to study it a little before putting it away. One useful purchase to make while in Korea is a small wallet, usually leather or eel-skin, in which to store both your own cards and those that you have collected. Another is a book to which you can transfer cards as your collection grows.

South Korean business cards can be very informative, with details of cell phones and e-mail, and picture cards are increasingly common. North Korean cards, by contrast, are pretty minimalist in the information that they convey: name, title, organization, and address, with a general telephone number, and possibly a fax number, for the organization. It is very difficult to obtain an individual number in North Korea. E-mail addresses are now beginning to appear. These will be of the organization rather than an individual. Sometimes an e-mail gets to the right person, sometimes it doesn't.

Because they attach importance to their own hierarchies, Koreans will also be interested in yours. Here the business card is very important, and it is a great mistake to try to operate without one. Put as much information as you can on yours. Koreans will eagerly seize on your business card, as it will, they hope, supply them with some clues about you and your status. Educational qualifications impress, especially if they come from a well-known establishment. Ranks and titles are also important, so if you can, add these to your business cards. In addition to what they can learn from your card, Koreans may well make detailed inquiries about your background, education, and beliefs. This is to be able to place you, to see where you might fit into their system.

Anything that seems confrontational should be avoided. Koreans tend to avoid too much eye contact. It is therefore regarded as somewhat rude to look straight into another person's eyes all the time while conversing. Koreans fix their gaze between the eyes and the nose of the other person and will often glance downward. Failure to "look somebody in the eye" is not considered a sign of weakness in Korea. Neither is it necessary to provide a "firm" handshake. Just a touch will do.

## PREPARATION

As with anywhere else, to conduct business successfully in either Korea requires a certain amount of forethought and planning. Read and study as much as you can in advance of beginning your efforts—such preparation is never wasted. Be patient, and do not expect speedy results. While contemporary South Korea often seems a place of great hustle and bustle, possessed of a "can-do" attitude, and in the North, too, you may be pushed for a quick decision, there is an older Korean tradition of not doing things in a hurry. It is wise to bear this in mind.

You should also be sure of what you want from your link with a Korean company and establish which companies might meet these needs. As far as South Korea is concerned, there is now a large amount of literature about Korean companies available both in print and electronic form. Information can also be gleaned from Chambers of Commerce and both South Korean and foreign embassies.

The South Korean business scene is somewhat more complicated than it was before the 1997 economic crisis. The crisis led to the breakup of the *chaebol*, or conglomerates, into separate companies, and to a large increase in foreign investment as areas hitherto closed off were opened up. The initial confusion has now settled down, but changes that have occurred mean that you may need to consider a wider group than might have been the case in the past.

### Perseverance

An essential element to conducting business in Korea is perseverance, both in presenting your case and in keeping up contacts with your Korean counterpart. Do not expect to conclude most business transactions in a single session. This may sometimes happen, but it is the exception. Rather, be prepared at the outset for a long haul. Expect to return to Korea more than once if your

business involves any form of long-term commitment.
By doing so, you show sincerity.

## NEGOTIATIONS

When in Korea, negotiate as the Koreans do. One
person, preferably the most senior, should carry out the
negotiations. Any others are there to advise (ideally in
writing), not to join in the discussion.

Actual negotiations are likely to take time, with
formal presentations being the order of the day.
Remember to allow time for interpretation. Many
Koreans will not be at ease with spoken English, even
if they can read it. Besides, interpretation allows both
sides time to think. Do not address your remarks to the
interpreter, however. Instead, while not staring directly
at him or her, make sure that you keep your eyes
toward your counterpart. Use titles such as chairman or
president instead of names alone; "Chairman Kim" is
better than "Mr. Kim" or "Madam Kim." Do not suggest
the use of given names. Koreans rarely do so among
themselves, and the chances are that you will end up
being addressed as "Mr. John" or "Madam Sarah," which
perhaps does not convey the message you wish to get
across. Curiously, the North may be a bit more relaxed
than the South in this matter. North Korean officials
seem to have no problem using foreigners' given names,
especially if they had known the person for a long time.

Do not give all your points away at the beginning.
Ideally, the foreign side should have its own dedicated

interpreter(s) to make sure that its case is really put across. In some cases, a native Korean speaker may tend to empathize with the Korean side rather than your own. Fortunately, this is not always the case, and it is also becoming easier to employ a non-native speaker as more institutions teach Korean to a high standard.

It is much better to let concessions or additional offers come out in the course of negotiations—that way, they seem more of a gain for the other side. Be less worried about reaching an agreed-upon document than about getting a broad and acceptable base on which to keep in contact. Contracts, even when signed, are not necessarily seen as the final word, but merely a stage, albeit a more definite stage, on the road to final agreement. If you cannot reach such agreement, make every effort to avoid a hostile break. If goodwill remains, it may be possible to come back to an issue after it has been reviewed.

Negotiations may go on late. Koreans generally work long hours, and do not expect to go home at the end of the formal working day. On some evenings, there may be formal dinners (you should reciprocate any such hospitality), followed by drinking and possibly singing. You can excuse yourself from drinking on health or religious grounds, but somebody on your side should be able to keep up with the Korean side.

It is best to avoid being humorous; jokes that need to go through an interpreter tend to fall flat, however good the joke or the interpreter. Remember also that Korean laughter will not always be related to humor; Koreans often laugh to hide embarrassment or to soften bad news, so be careful how you interpret their actions.

## BUSINESS ENTERTAINMENT

As well as formal dinners, which are usually held in upmarket restaurants, the Koreans also go in for informal post-work, or post-dinner, entertainment. This involves more food and very macho drinking rounds. *Poktanjoo* is a way of mixing whiskey and beer, and downing it in one go.

### The *Kisaeng* Party

At the apex of the entertaining world in South Korea are *kisaeng* houses, where well-trained women entertain customers. Like the *geisha* tradition in Japan, it derives from the Confucian idea that it is the duty of women to serve men in all things. Dinner in a *kisaeng* house, along with the subsequent drinking games, is an expensive undertaking, and foreigners are likely to find that invitations to such establishments are rare.

A typical *kisaeng* evening will involve much food and drink, with the girls (sometimes mature women) feeding their male companions and playing party games with them. There is also likely to be singing and dancing. Sometimes the entertainment is confined to traditional-style performances by the *kisaeng*, but nowadays the rest of the party are also likely to join in, in the style of a karaoke bar. While it is not unknown for a foreigner to organize a *kisaeng* party, it is wise to be guided by a Korean before attempting this.

Below the *kisaeng* house there is a variety of other establishments. "Salons" or cocktail lounges will provide female company in less exalted surroundings but can also be expensive. Salons may also be called "business clubs," but the service is the same. In all these establishments, if the chemistry and the cost is right, it may be possible to move on to more personal relations. But be warned, it is not part of the service as such.

### *Rare Entertainment*

Visiting the South Korean city of Kwangju, I took part in my only *kisaeng* party. As the evening progressed, the young lady looking after me, in addition to massaging my legs from time to time to an alarmingly high point on my thighs, kept offering me pieces of raw octopus that were still moving. I declined both the continuation of the massage and the octopus. Eventually, however, after a couple of hours, the octopus appeared not to be moving and so, when she picked up a piece with suckers on her chopsticks, I took it. It promptly grabbed the side of my mouth. Eventually I pried it off and swallowed it. My foreign colleague, a biologist by training, maintained that since it responded to stimuli and appeared to have the ability to move, it was alive.

### Karaoke

Most popular of all are karaoke bars. Karaoke has become a term so widely used in Korea that it can be considered part of the language. At a karaoke bar or room—the terms seem interchangeable—everybody in the party will be expected to sing, so the wise foreign visitor has a few songs prepared, whatever the state of his or (more rarely) her singing voice. Singing is so popular and widespread that you will encounter it on many other occasions as well. In good weather, many foreigners, even on short visits, find that they are invited to company or organization picnics, and these too provide an excuse for singing.

And visitors to North Korea need not think that they will escape. There are several karaoke establishments in Pyongyang and even run-down provincial hotels may have a karaoke room. The custom of calling for songs after dinner is well established among the ministries too, so however formal the diplomatic occasion, or the negotiations with the trade ministry, you are likely to be called on to sing in Pyongyang. And do not worry—however good or bad you are, there will certainly be a demand for an encore!

## GIFTS

Presents in the business context may be much larger than those given in the course of ordinary social contacts. Usually there will be a reciprocal exchange, which at least keeps the balance. Sometimes, however, the gift offered, and the gift expected, may be quite different. Perhaps the most sensible policy to follow is never to give more than you are happy with, whatever the hints and pressures from the other side.

## THE NORTH

Most of the above applies to South Korea, but much of it is also applicable to dealings with North Korea. The North may formally deny that it is a Confucian society but many "Confucian" traits still prevail, whether as respect for hierarchy or in attitudes toward women. In the North, entertainment may be less lavish and will not go on so long. However, it will form part of the business of doing business, as will the ability to match toast for toast and song for song. Gift giving, too, is important, although it is not always reciprocal. Again, you will find that the person who is clearly willing to remain engaged will be likely to succeed — "old friends" are valued. Be warned that contracts are even more likely to be but a stage in a process in the North.

In North Korea, people will be less familiar with Western ways than their counterparts in the South. Expectations can sometimes be very much out of line with reality. There is sometimes a tendency in North Korea to see things as a right rather than a possibility. North Korean negotiators can be very tough and demanding, and sometimes come across as very intimidating. The sense of isolation that many foreigners feel, cut off from sources of information and often kept apart from other foreigners, adds to the sense of intimidation, but firmness usually pays off.

There are many companies and individuals who have had business dealings with North Korea that have met both sides' needs. Be honest but careful, and make sure that a substantial portion of your payment comes before the completion of a deal, and you should be successful.

理而已。理既不二。則何得不與天
地鬼神同其用也。正音二十八字。
各象其形而制之。初聲凡十七字。
牙音「ㄱ」象舌根閉喉之形。舌音「ㄴ」
象舌附上腭之形。脣音「ㅁ」象口形。
齒音「ㅅ」象齒形。喉音「ㅇ」象喉形。
比「ㄱ」聲出稍厲。故加畫。「ㄴ」而「ㄷ」。「ㄷ」
而「ㅌ」。ㅁ而ㅂ。ㅂ而ㅍ。ㅅ而ㅈ。ㅈ而

# CHAPTER NINE

# COMMUNICATING

## LANGUAGE

An estimated 70 million people in the world speak Korean. The vast majority are on the Korean peninsula, but there are about 2.14 million in China, 2.1 million in the USA, 912,000 in Japan, and 500,000 in the former Soviet Union. The highest number in Europe is about 18,000 in Great Britain, including a small number from North Korea. Although there were many people of Korean ethnic origin in the Soviet Union, the language suffered badly during Stalin's time, and few now speak it. Outside these areas, Korean has not enjoyed the popularity of Chinese or Japanese, and relatively few non-Koreans know the language.

Most Westerners find Korean a difficult language. To the complexity of the grammar are added other factors that cause problems. Korean has absorbed many words of Chinese origin, which exist alongside native Korean words—both must be learned. Korean is a language with many levels of speech, with numerous honorifics depending on who is addressing whom, and in what context; there are at least nine degrees of respect or familiarity. In South Korea, a visitor who speaks some Korean will come in for much praise—only when one's language skills are really good will this praise disappear! In North Korea, while a little knowledge of Korean will earn similar plaudits, evidence of real language skills will be looked upon with suspicion, at least at first. Korean-speaking foreigners are seen as potential spies —particularly by older North Koreans who have had less exposure to Western or other cultures—and are not welcome.

Although all Koreans can communicate with each other, there are several distinct dialects. The political divide has led to each side stressing that "correct" speech is based around that of either Seoul or Pyongyang. Kim Il Sung condemned Seoul speech in the 1960s as being "firmly rooted in the rotten bourgeois life" of the past, full of loan words from Chinese, Japanese, and English, and overly feminine. In the South, North Korean speech is criticized for its heavy ideological content and for a deliberate break with the peninsula's past by stripping out Chinese-derived words. South Korea has a heavy influx of English-derived words as a result of a strong American presence since 1945, although even in the North, words such as camera, television, and hotel are in common use. It is possible that the influx of foreign words also affects the generations in South Korea; as elsewhere, older people profess themselves unable to understand the young. The latter pride themselves on being up-to-date in the "cool" language of international pop music and fashion.

### The Korean Alphabet

The written language as used in South Korea requires some knowledge of Chinese characters as well as of the Korean alphabet, although their use is steadily diminishing with the use of computers. Chinese characters are no longer in use in North Korea, though they can sometimes still be seen at historical sites or monuments. Kim Il Sung seems to have been proud of his Chinese calligraphy and wrote several inscriptions for buildings or places that he had caused to be restored.

The Korean alphabet is known as *Han'gul* in South Korea, and as *Choson muncha* in the North, and dates from the reign of King Sejong in the fifteenth century. In order to provide a means of writing more attuned to Korean grammar than Chinese ideographs, and that would be more generally accessible, he set teams of scholars to work on devising a new method of writing.

Today, all Koreans, North and South, are very proud of what they usually describe as the most scientific alphabet in the world, sometimes extending this to the language itself. The alphabet is simple to learn; an afternoon's assiduous work is all that is required to learn the individual letters, though much more is needed to be able to combine them properly, and to be aware of the subtle changes that take place in such combinations. Acquisition of the alphabet can help in traveling, since in some remote parts, romanized signs may be in short supply. It is also nice to be able to read slogans, even if they turn out to be saying no more than "Drink Coca-Cola."

There are a few traps for the foreigner. One is the "r" and "l" sounds, which, as in Japanese and Chinese, are almost interchangeable. There are also some differences in pronunciation between the northern and southern halves of the country—these have nothing to do with politics, however, and long predate the division of the peninsula. Thus, as already mentioned, the surname "Lee," "Li," "I," or "Yi," used in the south, is usually found as "Ree," "Rhee," or "Ri" in the north. Do not worry too much; Koreans will recognize it whichever way you pronounce it.

The language bears some similarity to those of neighboring countries. There are no definite or indefinite articles, grammatical number, or gender distinctions. Pronouns are rarely used, and sentences are often vague about the subject and tense of a verb. At the same time, while Korean contains many Chinese words, its grammar is very different. The grammar of Korean and Japanese is very similar, but the two languages sound very different. Korean appears to be linked to the Altaic group of languages, which includes Mongolian, Manchu, Hungarian, and Finnish, to name a few, but there is no clear evidence of any historical link between most of the languages so described. Certainly, if you speak Finnish or Hungarian, you will not find many opportunities to do so in Korea.

### Transliteration

How to romanize Korean has been a problem for Westerners since they first encountered the language in the seventeenth century. For a long time, French influence was strongest as a result of the nineteenth-century French Roman Catholic missionaries who worked (and in many cases, suffered martyrdom) in Korea. The French system of transliteration survives in the accepted spelling of Seoul. That, and a few other conventions, such as "Korea" spelt with a "C" will still be found in various Romance languages.

Two Americans devised the most widely used system of romanization in the late 1930s. George McAfee McCune (1908–48) was born in Pyongyang of missionary parents, while Edwin Oldfather Reischauer (1910–90) was a scholar of Japanese and later US ambassador to Japan. Working together with a group of Korean scholars, they created the McCune–Reischauer System, published by the Royal Asiatic Society Korea Branch in 1939. This system aimed to be a phonetic translation of modern Korean, using English consonants and Italian vowels, rather than a literal transcription of Han'gul. Its use spread rapidly. It has been used in South Korea from time to time, and, in a modified (and unacknowledged) version, it is still used in North Korea. Other systems in use include the Yale system, devised in the 1950s, which is much favored by linguists.

Many Koreans do not like the McCune–Reischauer System, however, since it does not exactly represent the Korean alphabet. Some Koreans appear to object because foreigners were involved in its development. Others have seen it as tainted by links with Japan, because of Reischauer's involvement. In South Korea, various attempts have been made to develop a more acceptable system, the latest of which was introduced in 2000, ousting McCune–Reischauer from all official publications, road signs, and similar material. Many English speakers do not like the new system because it throws up unfamiliar and unsightly combinations of letters and can lead to as many mispronunciations as McCune–Reischauer—the surname "Pak" (Park), for example, becomes "Bag"; "*tongnip*," independence, becomes "*dogrib*"; and the province of Cholla bukdo, "*Jeollabuk-do*." However, there is strong government pressure to use it and it is now ubiquitous in South Korea. No doubt, in time, it will all become as familiar as McCune–Reischauer, but it is a pity that romanization, one of the few points on which North and South have shared the same position, at least in recent years, has become another dividing point.

## FACE-TO-FACE

Communicating will generally not be too much of a problem, at least at a simple level. Koreans both North and South learn English from their schooldays onward, so in theory English is the most widespread second language on the peninsula—as French is in Britain. Remember that many Koreans never have the chance to use their foreign languages with native speakers, so they may well be shy of trying to talk to you. Persevere and your efforts may be rewarded. If you are not having much luck with the spoken language, try writing things down. Many people can read English even if they are nervous about speaking it.

If you have other languages, it may be worth trying them. Very old Koreans may still have some Japanese, for example, and most South Koreans will understand some written Chinese, since Chinese characters are still in use for some purposes. German and French will sometimes yield results. If all else fails, sign language may work!

In the North, you are unlikely ever to be left in circumstances where you do not have an English-speaking guide, and your guide will interpret most conversations. The quality of such interpretation varies, however, and at busy times when there are many foreign groups in town, you may find yourself with a guide whose command of English is not very good. Be patient if your meaning is not understood the first time. Remember that your guide will have had few opportunities to hear native English speakers.

## Nonconfrontation

Do not be surprised if there is a lack of eye contact during conversations, or indeed at other times. Koreans do not like to look directly at people except for the shortest periods, since this is regarded as confrontational. They are not being shifty, merely polite by Korean standards. Neither do they like to begin business right away. It is polite to exchange views about the weather or the season, and you may well be asked for your impressions of the country.

Koreans will also avoid confrontation in conversations or negotiations. The use of direct negatives is avoided; better to say, "There is a small problem," than to say "No." If there is a difficulty, like most people Koreans will become somewhat uneasy and may start shifting around—it is a good idea to suggest a break at such a point.

In South Korea, politics has become less of a taboo subject than it used to be but remember that the prevailing political ethos is very conservative by Western standards. Remember also that South Koreans are proud of the progress that they have made toward a more democratic society in recent years.

In the North, it is best to avoid political discussions. You will not get far, and if you are thought to be in any way critical, you may cause offense. In particular, you should avoid any hostile comment about Kim Il Sung, the founding president, his son Kim Jong Il, or the country's current leader Kim Jong Un. Any adverse comment will certainly be taken amiss, as will any mistreatment of pictures of the leaders. Do not deface or even crumple newspapers with their images. This has led to trouble for some visitors.

You will find that some subjects that might be avoided in the West will readily be brought into the conversation in Korea. Your health and married status may well become the subject of inquiry or debate in both North and South. In the South, be prepared for searching questions about your religion, especially from Korean Christians. You should also note that Korean Protestants do not generally smoke or drink, and that seeing foreign Protestants doing either may cause some disquiet.

Sports are a good conversational gambit, and inquiries about families are usually well received. Pictures of family members can be a help. Where and what you have studied will usually evoke a positive response. Remember, however, that most Koreans have only heard of a few educational establishments outside their own country. Harvard, Yale, Oxford, and Cambridge may be recognized, but not much beyond. Such topics, of course, belong at social rather than business gatherings.

## COMMUNICATIONS IN THE SOUTH

### The Press

Since the late 1980s, the South Korean press has been free of the political controls that operated during the years of military or quasi-military rule. Radio and television are perhaps not quite so free, but they are now much more willing to air controversial subjects, especially political ones, than was the case in the past.

Foreigners without Korean are well catered to, with two long-established English-language papers, the *Korean Herald* and the *Korean Times*. The former has long been seen as linked to the government, while the latter, a sister paper of the Korean *Hankook Ilbo* (*Korean Daily*), has been regarded as more independent. The reality is that it is hard to see much difference between them, either in coverage or in opinions. The Joongang Ilbo newspaper group has a link to the *International Herald Tribune*, and publishes a version of this. These papers provide both domestic and international stories, as well as information about theaters, lectures, and so on. They also have Internet sites. Foreign newspapers and magazines are widely available in Seoul and sometimes in the big hotels in other major cities.

## The Media

Television channels include the English-language "Arirang," which also has a Web page and an FM radio channel, and the American Forces Network, Korea (AFKN); the latter also runs a radio service.

The state Korean Broadcasting System (KBS) has radio stations that specialize in classical music. In the hotels, channels such as CNN and BBC World Television, and other European or American channels, will usually be available, as will Chinese and Japanese channels.

## The Internet

South Korea has the fastest Internet infrastructure in the world, and visitors will find that hotels are fully equipped for broadband access. Here, however, the government is inclined to be more interventionist than it is in the West, at least in regard to certain subjects.

Accessing Internet sites relating to North Korea is an offense under South Korea's national security laws, and some controversial political sites have been blocked.

For foreigners, there are many English-language sites giving information about developments in Korea and what is going on in the way of entertainment. There are also many foreign chat rooms and blogs available.

The overall impact of improved technologies in electronics and Internet speed has been to accelerate the changes in the way in which South Koreans interact socially, on a daily basis.

## Telephones, Smartphones, Apps

The South Korean fixed-line telephone system, run by another government monopoly, KT (formerly Korea Telecom), is equally efficient and widespread throughout the country. All hotels are on IDD.

South Korea has taken to cell phones in a big way, and two of the world's main manufacturers, LG and Samsung, are South Korean. KT is the main provider. Visitors will find that acquiring and operating a cell phone is easy and useful. In early 2019, South Korea became the first country to roll out a fifth generation, 5G, mobile wireless service, built into the newly released Samsung smartphone.

Cell phones have become a huge part of everday life, especially among the young. Smartphones are used for activities such as banking, making payments, including public travel passes and bills, and communications. The "digital wallet" is the new norm, and cash rarely changes hands. Samsung has invented a payment app for public use called Samsung Pay. This stores personal banking information securely and allows personal payments to be made in real-time. Payment for taxi rides, public transportation, and utility bills can be transacted with the press of a button. The downside is that it is a built-in app exclusively for Samsung cell phones. However, there are alternatives. Kakaotalk is a communication app developed primarily to offer most of the services that Samsung Pay provides. It has introduced a payment and banking service through its sub function within the same app called Kakaopay. Kakaotaxi is another dedicated function for calling taxis, the Korean equivalent of UBER.

### Mail

The modern Korean postal system dates from the 1880s; a famous political event is the so-called "Post Office coup of 1884," when progressive politicians were attacked while attending a dinner marking the opening of the country's first Post Office. The modern government-owned Korea Post provides an efficient system, with cards and letters reaching the United States and Europe within a couple of days of mailing. The Post Office is also conscientious about returning undelivered mail.

## COMMUNICATIONS IN THE NORTH

The picture is different in North Korea. The press, radio, and television are tightly controlled, and are only available in Korean. The weekly *Pyongyang Times* newspaper, which appears in English and a number of other languages, contains no practical information about what is happening in North Korea. Instead, readers receive a stream of propaganda articles that quickly begin to pall. For information on theaters or the circus, visitors need to ask their guides. However, foreigners in some hotels in Pyongyang today can view BBC World Service Television and some Chinese channels, including Chinese Central Television's English-language channel. What is available often varies, perhaps depending on who is staying in the hotel on any given day.

The postal system appears efficient, although delays sometimes occur because of the relatively low number of international flights from the North. The telephone and fax systems provide international direct dialing and generally work well, although poor electricity supplies can interrupt transmission. Telephone directories may exist, but they appear to be treated as state secrets. They are not available to foreigners. Foreign embassies, international organizations, and foreign companies do not have access to the telephone network used by Koreans. The network they use has the area code 381, which also gives access to the main hotels, Air Koryo, and, to a limited extent, some ministries.

Access to the Internet in North Korea is very limited. For some years, North Korean sponsored sites based in China, Japan, and Germany provided some contact, and from about 2009 a number of sites have emerged in North Korea. Some e-mail addresses have also become known. Resident foreigners often do have access to the Internet and some visitors may do so.

For a brief period in 2002, foreigners could bring in cell phones, even though they could not be used. This seemed to be in anticipation of the introduction of a domestic mobile system. This was introduced in 2003, but it closed down in June 2004. Foreign cell phones again were taken away on entry and returned on departure. A new domestic cell phone system began in 2009, run by an Egyptian company. By early 2012, it was said to have over a million subscribers and to be available throughout the country. Neither handsets nor calls are cheap. The network is available to foreigners, whether residents or visitors, but, as with landlines, there is no access to the system used by most Koreans. Foreigners can again bring in cell phones, but these do not work in the DPRK.

## CONCLUSION

Here is a peninsula of spectacular natural beauty that matches anything in the world. Seoul or Pyongyang may not have many historical remains, but both reward their visitors in different ways. A cultural center in its own right, Korea has also played a major role in forging links between mainland and island East Asia. It was the channel for, and the interpreter of, Chinese culture for Japan. Its pottery has been the envy of both Chinese and Japanese potters since the tenth century.

Modern Korea has seen two very different political and economic experiments. South Korea's development has been astounding, as a visit to its vibrant cities and modern industrial complexes will quickly demonstrate. North Korea is in some ways equally remarkable, as one of the few surviving relics of the Marxist–Leninist experiment that began in Russia in 1917, but which here has developed in very different ways.

The Koreans are well worth getting to know better. These are tough people who have resisted all attempts by powerful neighbors to dominate them or take over their territory. They can come across as determined and firm, but they respond well to the hand of friendship. Whether North or South, Koreans take to those who persist in getting to know them. Go frequently, and before long you are an old friend, entitled to special consideration. They will be demanding, sometimes overwhelmingly so, but if they believe that you are on their side, they will do everything possible to help you.

# FURTHER READING

Bandi. *The Accusation: Forbidden Stories from Inside North Korea*. London: Serpent's Tail, 2017.

Breen, Michael. *The Koreans: Who They Are, What They Want, Where Their Future Lies*. London: Orion Business Books, 1998.

Crowder Han, Suzanne. *Notes on Things Korean*. Seoul, and Elizabeth, NJ: Hollym, 1996.

Cumings, Bruce. *Korea's Place in the Sun: A Modern History*. New York and London: W. W. Norton, 1997.

——. *North Korea: Another Country*. New York and London: The New Press, 2004.

Hoare, James. *Historical Dictionary of the Republic of Korea*. Lanham, MD, and London: Rowman and Littlefield, 4th edition, 2021.

——. *Historical Dictionary of the Democratic People's Republic of Korea*. Lanham, MD, and London: Rowman and Littlefield. 2nd edition, revised and expanded, 2019.

Hoare, James, and Susan Pares. *Conflict in Korea: An Encyclopedia*. Santa Barbara, CA, Denver, CO, and Oxford: ABC-CLIO, 1999.

Horlyck, Charlotte. *Korean Art: From the 19th Century to the Present*. London: Reaktion Books, 2017.

Kohls, L. Robert. *Learning to Think Korean: A Guide to Living and Working in Korea*. Yarmouth, ME: Intercultural Press, 2001.

Lee, Ki-baik. *A New History of Korea*. Translated by Edward Willet Wagner, with Edward J. Schultz. Cambridge, MA, and London: Harvard University Press, 1984.

Oberdorfer, Don, and Robert Carlin. *The Two Koreas: A Contemporary History*. New York: Basic Books, 3rd ed., revised and updated, 2014.

Portal, Jane. *Art and Archaeology of Korea*. London: British Museum Press, 2000.

Pratt, Keith, and Richard Rutt. *Korea: A Historical and Cultural Dictionary*. Richmond, Surrey: Curzon Press, 1999.

Springer, Chris. *Pyongyang: The Hidden History of the North Korean Capital*. Budapest: Entente Bt., 2003.

Tudor, Daniel. *Korea: The Impossible Country*. Tokyo: Tuttle, 2012.

Tudor, Daniel, and James Pearson. *North Korea Confidential,* Tokyo: Tuttle, 2015.

Willoughby, Robert. *North Korea: The Bradt Travel Guide*. Chalfont St. Peter, Bucks, UK: Bradt Travel Guides, 3rd ed., 2014.

# PICTURE CREDITS

Cover image: *Temple in the grounds of Kyongbok Palace, Seoul* / Pixabay.

Pixabay: page 12 by hiking.

Canva: pages 21 by praditp; 42, 126 by Reabirdna; 80 by efired; 94 by gyro; 112 by Busan Drone; 120 by davidfranklin.mail; 136, 151, 156 by aaron90311; 195 by robertcicchetti.

Images on the following pages reproduced under Korean Open Government License Type 1: Attribution: 60, 122 ©국립중앙박물관 (National Museum of Korea).

Images on these pages reproduced under Creative Commons Attribution-Share Alike 4.0 International license: 56, 114 (top) © Chaicat; 66 (top) © Jhcbs1019; 72 © Ken Eckert; 104 © Fun한여자; 139 © Minseong Kim.

Reproduced under Creative Commons Attribution-Share Alike 3.0 Unported license: 34, 131 © Bjørn Christian Tørrissen; 74 © Robert at Picasa; 82 © Adbar; 86–7 © ຮ່ຳພນຫອງໄຖ໌ອຸຍ; 96 © GFDL; 98 © OlkhichaAppa; 101 © by World to Table at Flickr; 115 © Steve46814; 117 © by bdnegin (Brian Negin); 149 © Gilad Rom; 162 © Bohao Zhao.

Creative Commons Attribution-Share Alike 2.5 Generic license: 58 © 대한민국 정부 문화체육관광부 문화재청.

Creative Commons Attribution-Share Alike 2.0 Generic license: 17 © Martin Chen; 23 © Republic of Korea; 33 ©Roman Harak; 47 © Matt Scott; 61, 63 © by joonghijung ay Flicker; 66 (bottom), 116, 118, 119 © Korea.net (http://www.korea.net) / Korean Culture and Information Service (Jeon Han); 73 © hojusaram; 75 © Ver Villa; 99 © Chloe Lim; 100 © L. W. Yang; 110 © by m-louis; 114 (bottom) © by ddol-mang; 132–3 © Laika ac from USA.

Creative Commons CC0 1.0 Universal Public Domain Dedication: 7 © Gringer; 124 © Brücke-Osteuropa.

Open Government Licence version 1.0: 165 © Foreign and Commonwealth Office.

Adobe Stock: page 85 © By DragonImages.

# INDEX